EASY PIANO

Uplifting Inspiring Songs

FOR KIDS

ISBN 978-1-70515-640-7

HAL•LEONARD®

Visit Hal Leonard Online at
www.halleonard.com

World headquarters, contact:
Hal Leonard
7777 West Bluemound Road
Milwaukee, WI 53213
Email: info@halleonard.com

In Europe, contact:
Hal Leonard Europe Limited
42 Wigmore Street
Marylebone, London, W1U 2RN
Email: info@halleonardeurope.com

In Australia, contact:
Hal Leonard Australia Pty. Ltd.
4 Lentara Court
Cheltenham, Victoria, 3192 Australia
Email: info@halleonard.com.au

Contents

Song Notes

A - You're Adorable

This adjective-filled alphabet song from the late 1940s has been sung by many artists and celebrities over the years, including Perry Como, Captain Picard of Star Trek fame, and the Muppets! You'll want to "swing" the eighth notes in the melody as indicated by this sign (♪♪ = ♪♪) next to the tempo. Instead of straight eighths, play the eighth notes with a swinging, long-short feel for just the right amount of bouncy jazz.

Beautiful Day

Sung by the band U2, this 2001 GRAMMY® Song of the Year has an upbeat feel and a positive message. The group's lead singer Bono has said the song is about finding joy. The lyrics fall naturally in the syncopated melody, so singing along can help you learn this song. Notice that when both hands play at the same time they often play the same rhythm. The opening bars repeat throughout; noticing this is also a key to putting the song together. Let's get right to it because "…it's a beautiful day, don't let it get away."

Better When I'm Dancing

Meghan Trainor wrote and performed this peppy dance tune in 2015 for *The Peanuts Movie*. Use the lyrics to build your confidence with the dotted eighth-sixteenth-note rhythm throughout this song. You'll see this rhythm in both left hand and right hand. Start with the left hand in bar 5. Set a strong quarter-note pulse and count "1-ee-and-a," playing on beat one, and again on the "a," the fourth of the four sixteenths. Go ahead and accent that last sixteenth tied into the next beat. Now, study the right-hand rhythm in bar 8. Once you're comfortable with this rhythm the rest of the song is a breeze!

Brave

Written and performed by Sara Bareilles, this inspiring pop hit made the Top 40 in 2013. Choose a moderate tempo, keeping the groove going while allowing the lyrics to shine. This song reminds us to be who we are and speak with confidence. The chord progression C-Am-F-G repeats throughout, making this an easy song to learn. The left hand plays single notes, allowing you to focus on the rhythm of the melody. Sing along! Be brave!

Can't Stop the Feeling!

Justin Timberlake wrote this funky disco-pop tune for the 2016 *Trolls* movie soundtrack. Set an energetic tempo right from the beginning. The harmony is built on a simple chord progression (C-Am7-F-Am7) but sometimes the F chord in the progression is an Fmaj9 (see bar 3) which is an F chord (F-A-C) with an added G. Notice the sound when playing F and G together. Other times, the F chord is an Fmaj7, (see bar 7) which is an F chord with an added E. Here again is another colorful sound, F and E played together. Don't shy away from the dissonance this creates and have fun with the changing harmonies.

Cupid Shuffle

Performed by the rapper Cupid, this 2007 hit generated a popular line dance. You'll notice that the left-hand part provides an easy but essential bass line to this repetitive melody. If you're playing for the dancers, keep a steady but bouncy tempo with enough energy to keep things moving. If you're dancing, just follow the directions in the song's lyrics, "to the right, to the right," "to the left, to the left," and so on. Go on now, get "down, down, do your dance."

Firework

Katy Perry's inspirational lyrics and dance pop vibe helped this 2010 song rise to #1 on the Billboard Hot 100. The left-hand part really drives this arrangement, and for the first half of the song you'll be playing 5ths. What makes this easy is that the 5ths stay close together on the keyboard. Notice the bass notes fall into this pattern: C-B♭-A-F. Practice those four bars until they are easy to play. At the sign 𝄋 left hand changes to repeated eighth notes, and the pattern changes slightly as well: C-D-A-F. Once you've learned left hand, add right-hand melody, and don't forget to sing along!

Happy

This catchy and multiple award-winning tune was written by Pharrell Williams. As the one and only song on the *Despicable Me 2* soundtrack, it also has the distinction of being the most successful song of 2014. Have fun with the jaunty bass line beginning in bars 4-5. This little riff appears three times in a row, creating an up-tempo soul feel. Enjoy the challenge of playing two parts at the same time beginning with the pickup to bar 18, "Because I'm happy," followed by "Clap along…" Play each part separately and you'll notice it's quite simple. Take an extra bit of effort to get the timing just right, counting eighth notes through the bar. For even more challenge, sing the right-hand part as you play both parts, then switch, and sing the left-hand part!

I Love

Sometimes called the "little baby duck song" because of the opening lyric, this 1973 favorite by Tom T. Hall includes something for everyone to love. The simple, gentle melody is harmonized with just three chords, so you'll have this country tune under your fingers in no time. Check out the "walking" bass line beginning in bar 12. Starting with left-hand C, the bass notes "walk" down the scale: B♭ in the next measure, A in the next, down to G. Play this classic for someone you love.

Lead the Way

Sung during the end credits of the 2021 Disney animated film *Raya and the Last Dragon*, "Lead the Way" is the theme song for an epic adventure. The harmonic structure is simple, just four chords: F-B♭-Dm-Csus (C major chord with an added F). The bass notes in the left hand have a repetitive rhythm and the right-hand melody is syncopated. Counting steady eighth notes throughout the bar will "lead the way" to where the syncopated notes should fall.

Mah-Nà Mah-Nà

This fun novelty song was first heard in the 1960s and became popular around the world, most notably in the U.S. on *The Muppet Show* television series. There are no actual words, just nonsense syllables and improvised scat singing. If you're unfamiliar with scat singing check out the many recorded versions of this catchy tune and have a go at some scat singing yourself. Beginning in bar 7 the diagonal lines between the staves show the melody moving from bass to treble clef. Watch out for the added sharps and naturals. Remember that a sharp raises a note a half step, and the natural cancels the sharp. For example, in bar 7 you'll play G♯ in the bass clef, but G♮ in the treble clef!

Me and Julio Down by the Schoolyard

Written by Paul Simon in 1972, this rhythmic story-song makes everyone want to get up and dance. The meaning of the song has often been up for debate, but Simon has remained vague. We may never know "what the mama saw," but regardless, have fun with this song! The opening bars mimic the guitar riff in the original recording. Choose a tempo that moves along but still gives you time to fit in all the lyrics. Notice in bars 5-6-7 the time signature changes from 𝄴 to 𝟤𝟦 and back to 𝟦𝟦. That happens several more times, but it's not as tricky as it looks. The quarter note stays the same throughout, so if you keep a steady pulse, you'll have no problem.

Over the Rainbow

A classic ballad loved by many, "Over the Rainbow" was written for the 1939 film *The Wizard of Oz* and was sung by Judy Garland in the role of Dorothy. The song begins with an introductory verse, and right from the beginning notice the long melodic line arching over four bars at a time. Play with *legato*, connecting each note smoothly to the next. Look out for accidentals (sharps and flats not found in the key signature) and sink into those notes. Emphasize the dissonance and relax into the resolution of these colorful harmonies.

Pollywog in a Bog

If you haven't already, check out the music video for this selection from *Snacktime*, Barenaked Ladies' 2009 Juno Award-winning Children's Album of the Year. Play along with fox, flying squirrel, otter, possum, and owl as they tell the story of their friend the pollywog. To begin, focus on the groovy left-hand riff. Spend some time getting comfortable with the opening four-bar intro and bars 5-8 (repeated for the first section of the song) before you add the right-hand melody. There's a key change at bar 35, moving from G major to C major—now all Fs are no longer sharp.

Remedy

From the 2015 album *25*, Adele has said that "Remedy" was inspired by her son and sung "for everyone I really love." This beautiful piano ballad has an almost waltz-like quality. The time signature is $\frac{6}{8}$, but there is a subtle "1-2-3" movement overall. Considering the lyrics will help you decide on just the right tempo, so don't be afraid to sing along to achieve a sense of flow and bring the message of this song to life.

Rescue

From the 2019 album, *Look Up Child*, singer/songwriter Lauren Daigle describes this song as very personal, and hopes the lyrics convey the message that while you may be struggling, there are better days ahead. Written in $\frac{6}{8}$, choose a slower feel of two beats per bar with a dotted quarter-note pulse. As the lyrics enter, don't let the ledger lines in right hand confuse you. Use Middle C as your landmark, and determine the ledger line note based on its distance from Middle C. There's a tricky rhythm in right hand that first appears in bars 13-14. Notated as dotted eighth followed by sixteenth tied to eighth, another way to think about it is two dotted eighths. Play two equal beats per pulse. If in doubt, listen to Lauren Daigle's recorded version. Once you can hear and feel the rhythm, it will be easy to play each time it appears throughout the song.

Respect

Otis Redding is credited with writing the first version of "Respect" in 1965, but it's Aretha Franklin's 1967 rearranged version (including the added R-E-S-P-E-C-T chorus) that became one of the most famous R&B hits of all time. This iconic anthem to human dignity has a bounce and swagger that needs to be played with a bit of attitude. While the left hand plays a steady beat in the bass, the melody is more conversational, so punctuate those short phrases to get the message of the lyrics across. Play the chorus with all the confidence and respect you can muster!

Theme from Spider Man

Recognized as Spidey's official theme song, this instantly recognizable tune was written for the famous 1967 TV cartoon. The syncopated melody gives this tune its signature superhero drive. You'll notice the eighth note tied to quarter-note rhythm in almost every bar. Don't be afraid to lean into that rhythm, but keep the tempo moving. Land on the final Dm$\frac{6}{9}$ chord (D minor chord with B and E added) with some extra energy for a dissonant and foreboding ending!

This Is Me

This dramatic anthem is from the 2017 movie musical *The Greatest Showman*. There are many patterns and repetitions throughout, which help build momentum as you tell the story of what it means to embrace yourself as you are. Beginning with the very first bar of introduction, the left-hand bass notes move B-C♯-D, immediately repeated an octave higher, notated in treble clef. This signature motive is repeated throughout—again in bars 5-6, 9-10, 14-15, and continuing. Choose a tempo that moves along but gives you time to articulate the lyrics clearly.

Wake Me Up!

Swedish DJ and record producer Avicii wrote this #1 dance single in 2013. It went on to be the highest charting dance track of the decade 2010-2019. Learning the repetitive chord progression will help you get into the spirited groove of this song. The chord pattern Am-F-C-G begins with the verse (bar 5), with only a slight change to Am-F-C-E in the chorus (see the chord change to E in bar 24). Once your left hand knows its way around, add right-hand melody for a fun spin on the dance floor.

You'll Sing a Song and I'll Sing a Song

Written by Ella Jenkins and often recognized as her signature song, this 1966 classic is an example of call-and-response singing. The leader sings the verse alone the first time, with everyone joining at the repeat. Continuing, the leader may only sing the first phrase or two before everyone joins in. Ella Jenkins is a leading composer/performer of children's music, winning a Grammy Lifetime Achievement Award in 2004. She's an influential supporter of children, parents, and caregivers all over the world.

You're My Best Friend

This up-tempo Queen favorite was written by John Deacon, the band's bass player, in 1975. When he wrote it, Deacon played the song on the electric piano, an instrument Freddie Mercury refused to play. So, the song has been performed and recorded both ways, with electric piano played by Deacon and vocals by Mercury, and with Freddie on grand piano and vocals. Whichever instrument you use, keep a swing feel going throughout. Really dig into those repeated low C notes in left hand to set the tone both rhythmically and energetically. Lean into the syncopated chords in the ending bars to keep that energy going until the last note.

A – You're Adorable

Words and Music by BUDDY KAYE,
SIDNEY LIPPMAN and FRED WISE

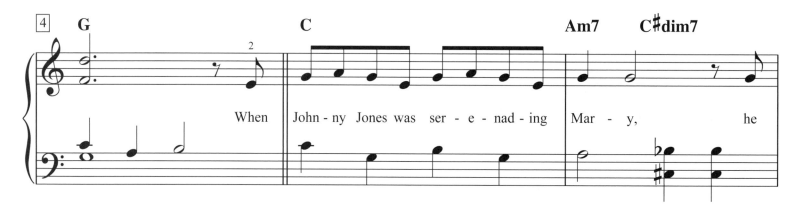

When John - ny Jones was ser - e - nad - ing Mar - y, he

sure could quote a lot of po - et - ry. But he'd much rath - er tell her what he

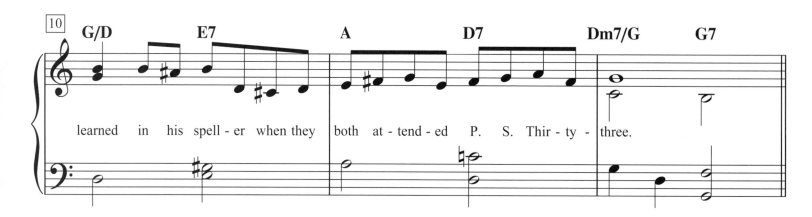

learned in his spell - er when they both at - tend - ed P. S. Thir - ty - three.

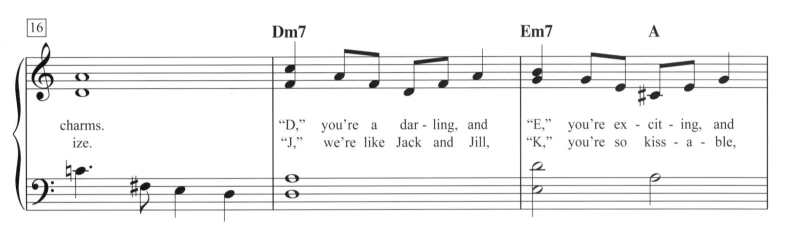

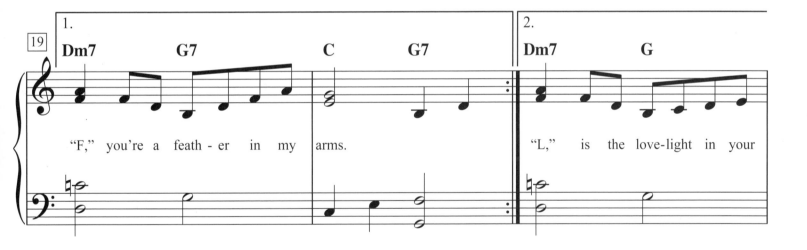

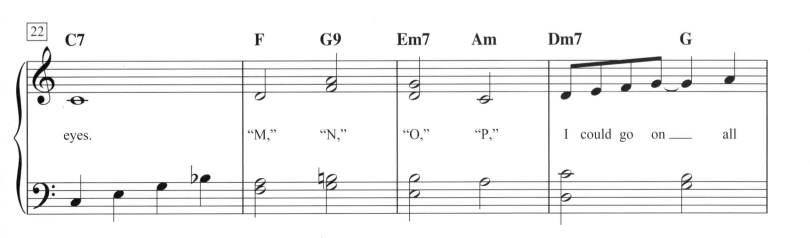

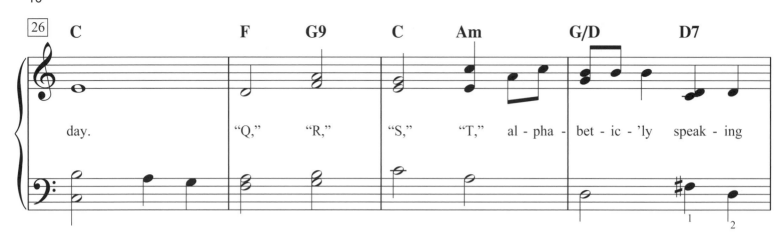

day. "Q," "R," "S," "T," al-pha-bet-ic-'ly speak-ing

you're o-kay! __ "U," made my life com-plete, "V" means you're ver-y sweet,

dou-ble "U," "X," "Y," "Z." It's fun to wan-der through the

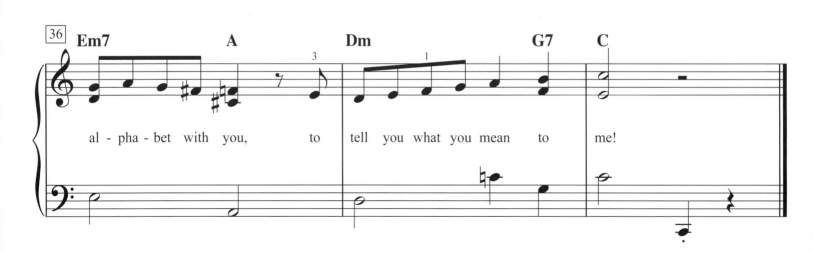

al-pha-bet with you, to tell you what you mean to me!

Beautiful Day

Words by BONO
Music by U2

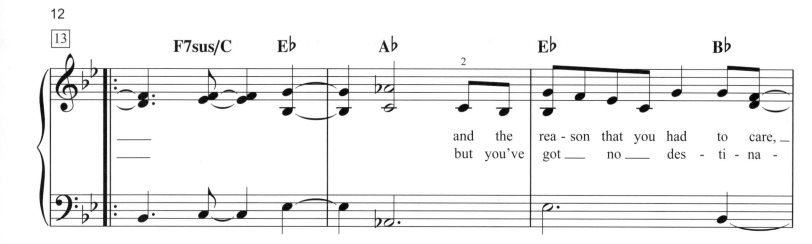

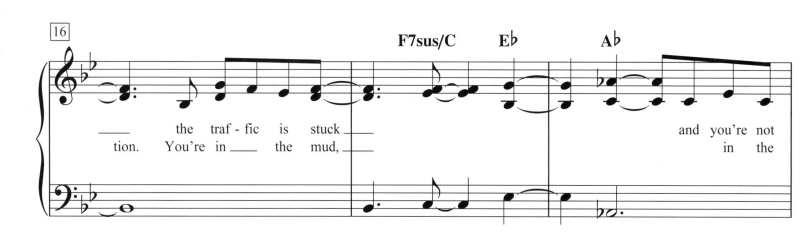

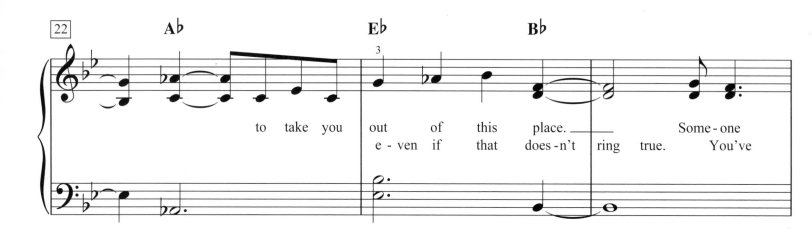

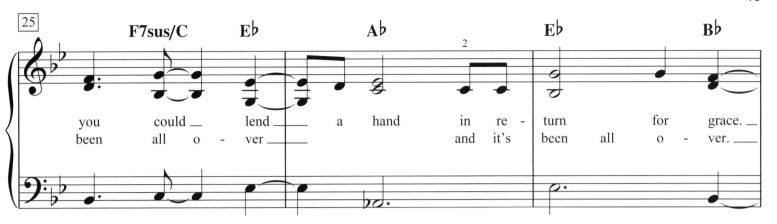

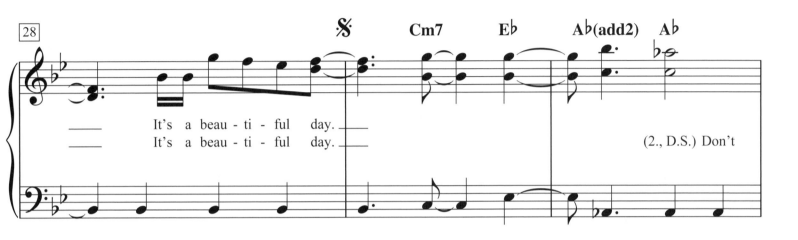

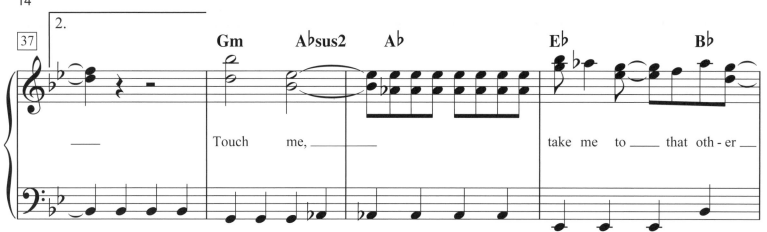

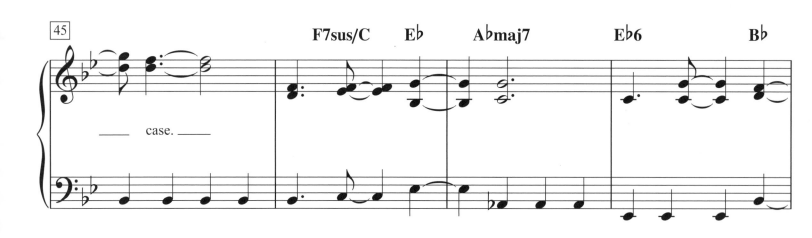

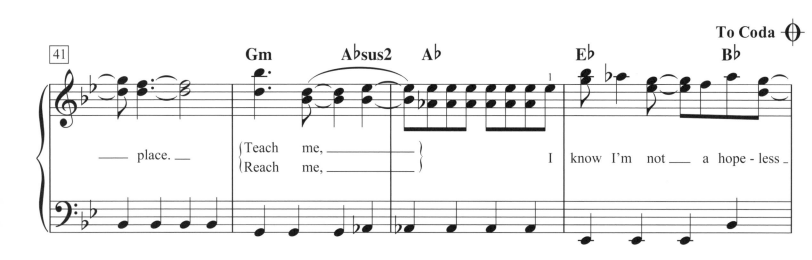

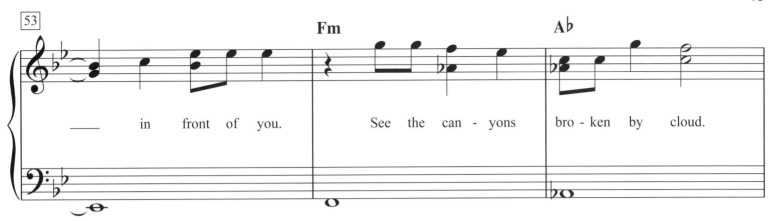

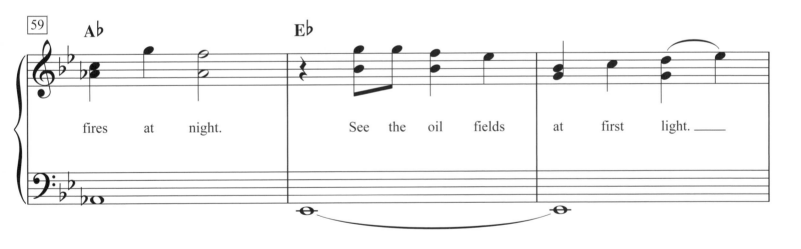

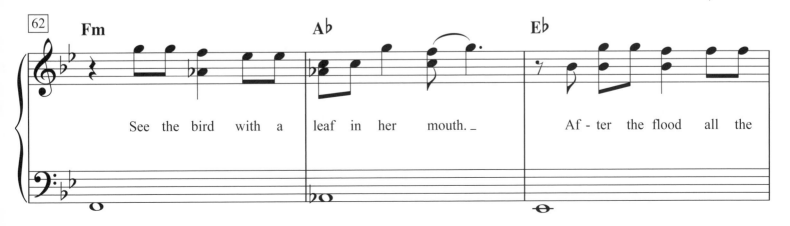

col - ors came out.

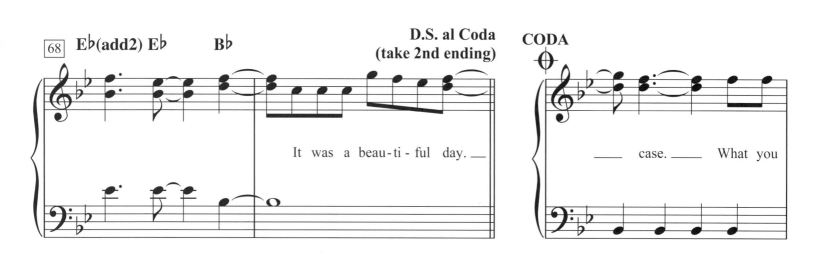

It was a beau-ti-ful day. ___

___ case. ___ What you

don't have, you don't need it now. ___ What you don't know, you can feel ___

___ it some-how. What you don't have, you don't ___ need it now. ___ You don't

need it now. _____ It's a beau-ti-ful day.

rit.

Cupid Shuffle

Words and Music by
BRYSON BERNARD

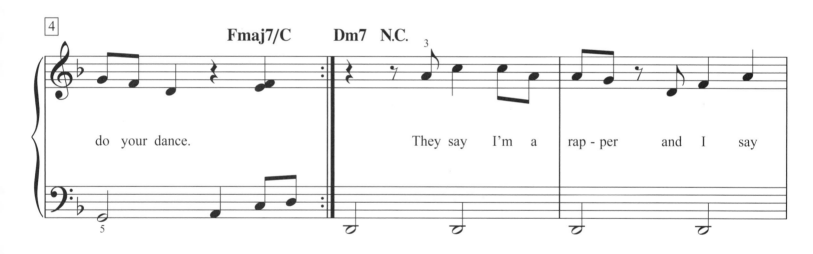

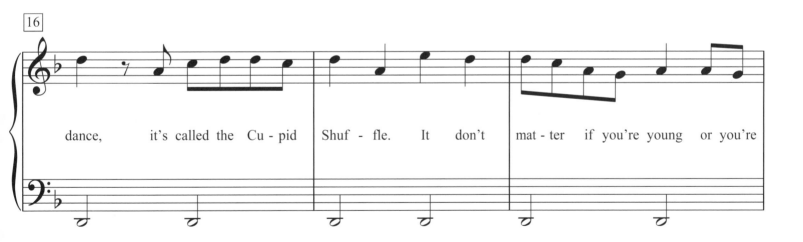

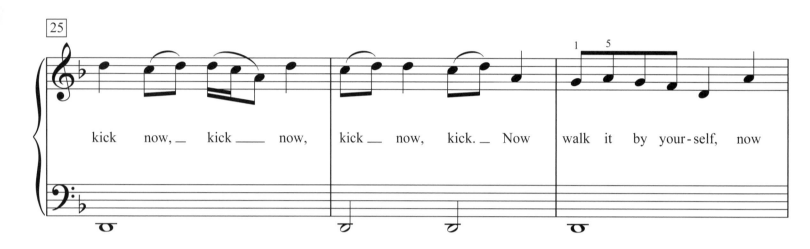

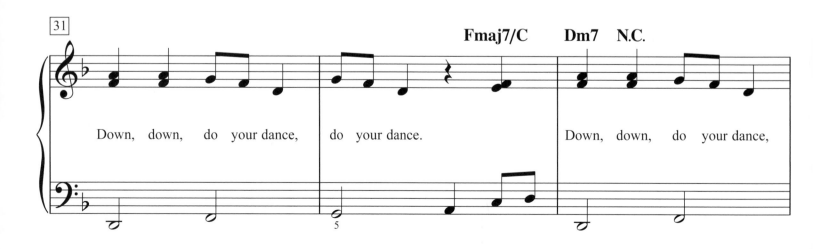

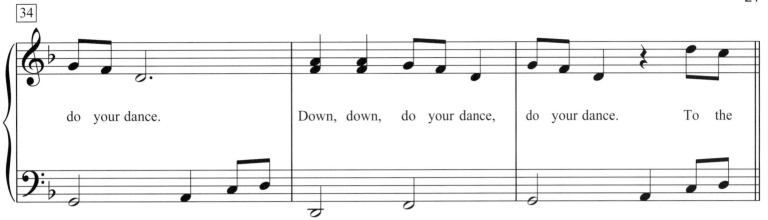

do your dance. | Down, down, do your dance, do your dance. To the

right, to the right, to the right, to the right. To the left, to the left,___ to the

left, to the left. Now kick now,__ kick___ now, kick__ now, kick.__ Now

walk it by your-self, now | walk it by your-self. To the | walk it by your-self.

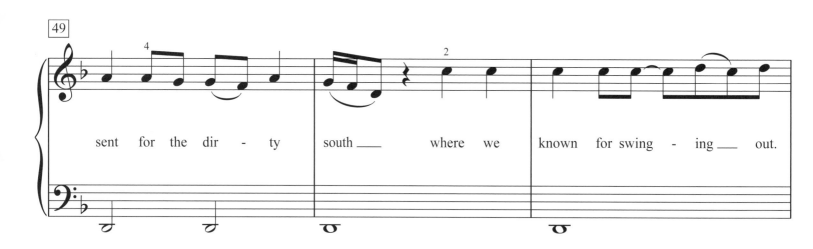

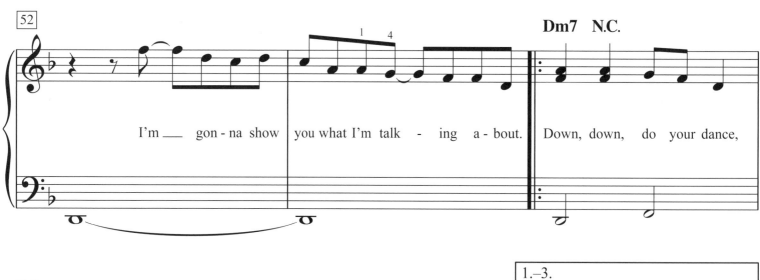

do your dance.   To the   right,   the right,   the   right, the right, the right.   The

left,   the left,   the   left, the left, the left. Now   kick   now, kick   now,

come   on   ba - by kick.   Now   walk   it   by   your - self,   walk

it   by your - self. To the   it   by your - self and do the   Cu - pid   Shuf - fle.

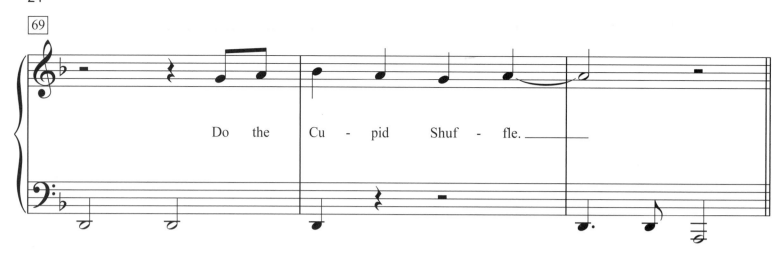

Do the Cu - pid Shuf - fle. ____

Down, down, do your dance, do your dance. Down, down, do your dance,

do your dance. Down, down, do your dance, do your dance.

Down, down, do your dance, do your dance.

Better When I'm Dancin'

from THE PEANUTS MOVIE

Words and Music by MEGHAN TRAINOR
and THADDEUS DIXON

Moderately fast

Don't think a - bout it,
When you fi - n'lly let go,

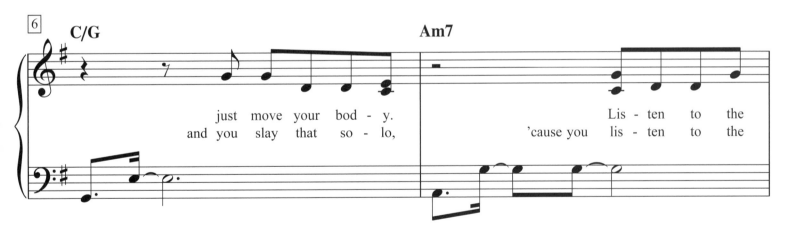

just move your bod - y.
and you slay that so - lo,

Lis - ten to the
'cause you lis - ten to the

mu - sic, ___ sing, "Oh aye ___ oh."
mu - sic, ___ sing - in', "Oh aye ___ oh."

Just move those left feet.
'Cause you're con - fi - dent, babe,

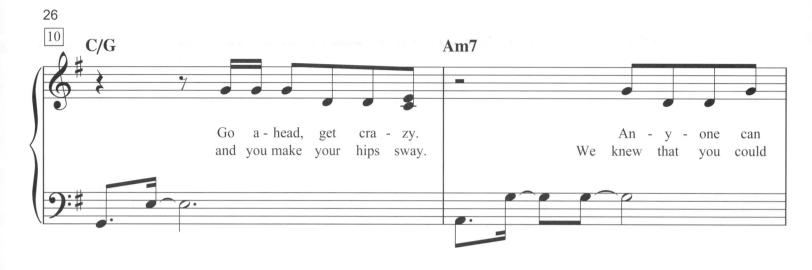

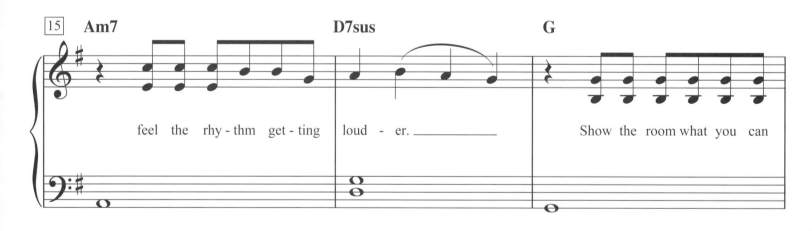

27

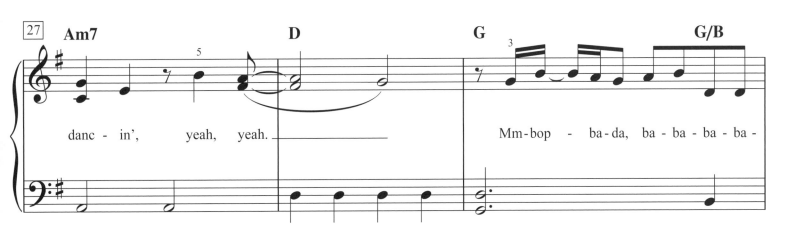

28

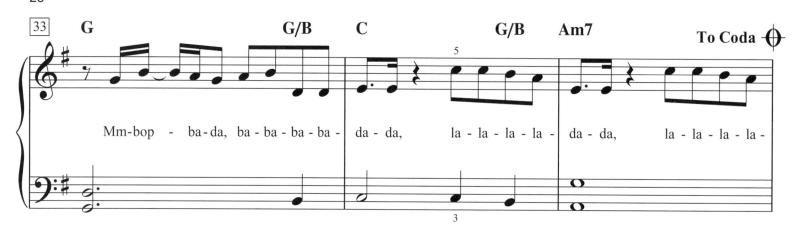

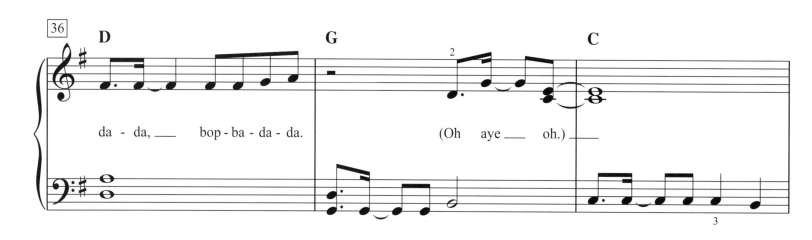

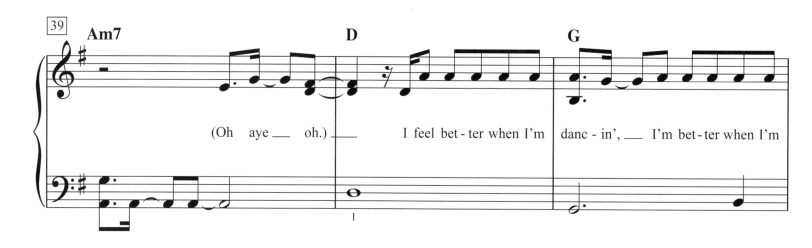

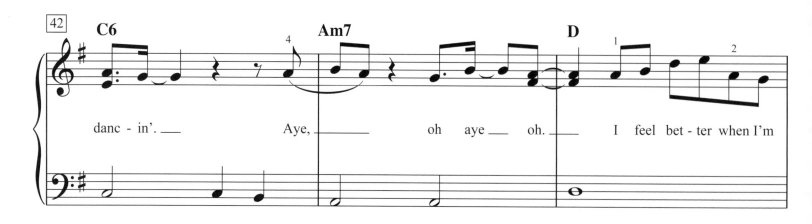

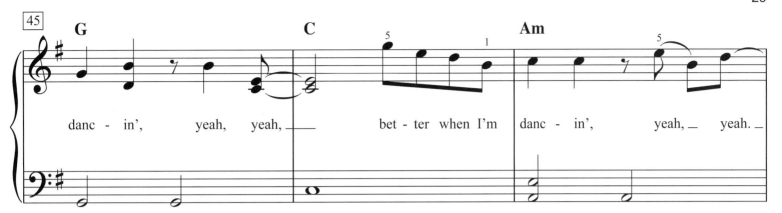

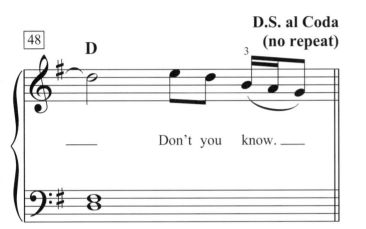

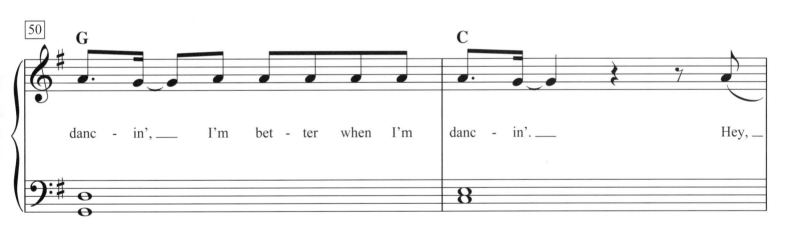

Brave

Words and Music by SARA BAREILLES
and JACK ANTONOFF

You can be a-maz-in', you can turn a phrase __ in-to a wea-pon or a

drug. You can be the out-cast __ or be the back-lash of some-bod-y's lack of

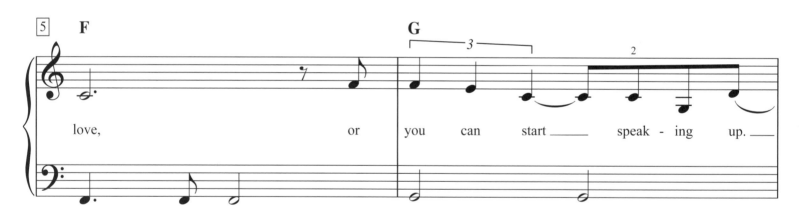

love, or you can start __ speak-ing up. __

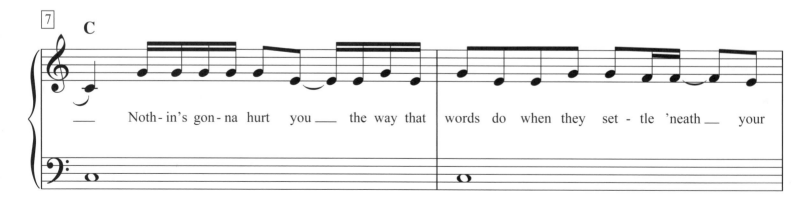

__ Noth-in's gon-na hurt you __ the way that words do when they set-tle 'neath __ your

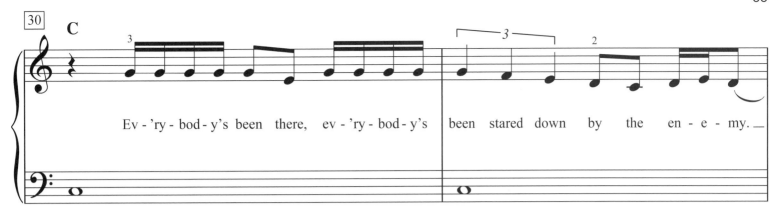

34

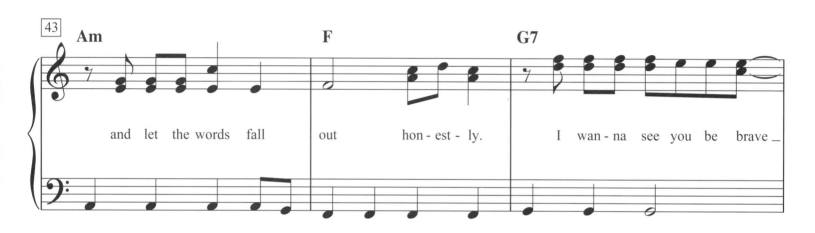

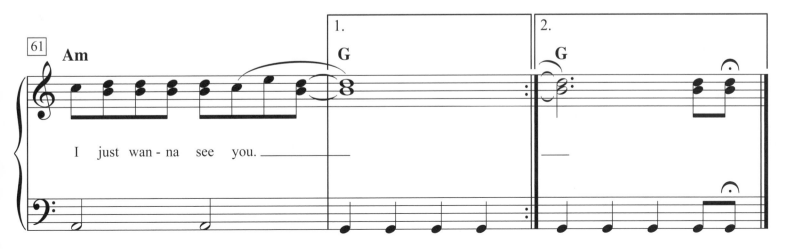

Can't Stop the Feeling!

from TROLLS

Words and Music by JUSTIN TIMBERLAKE,
MAX MARTIN and SHELLBACK

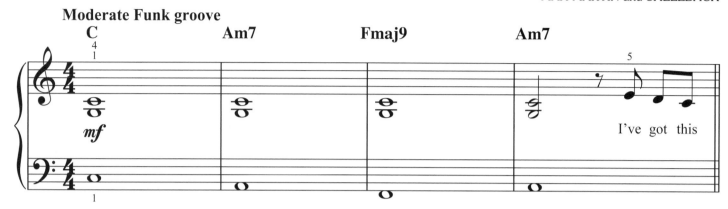

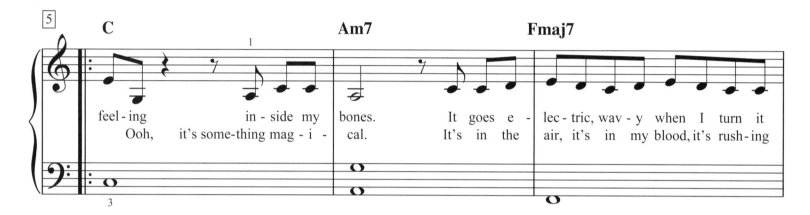

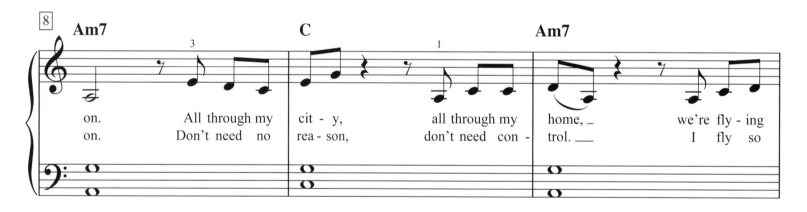

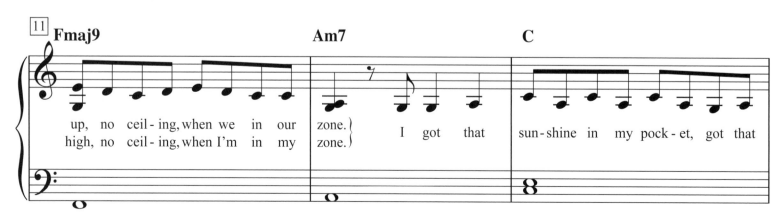

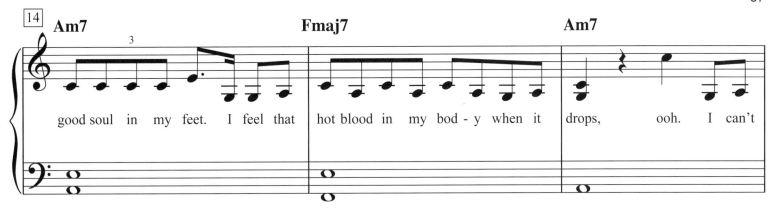

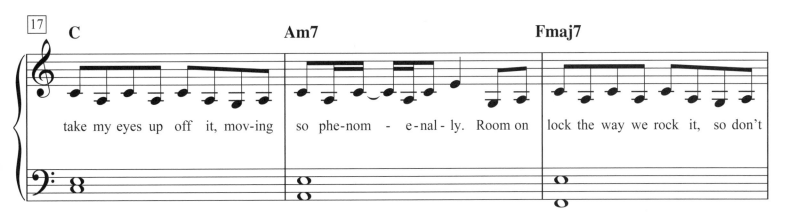

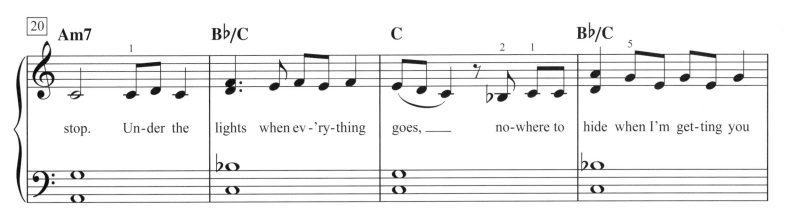

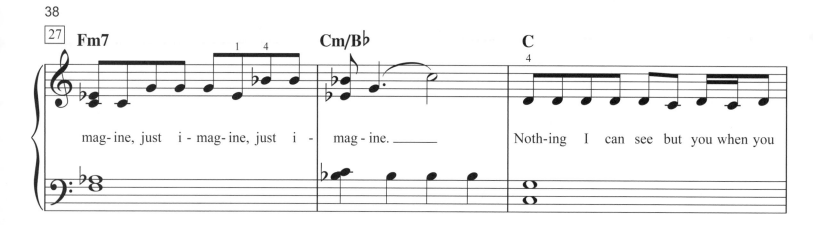

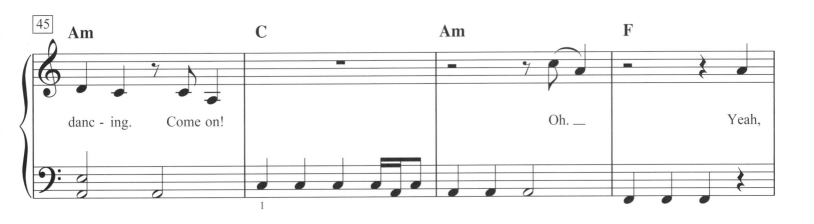

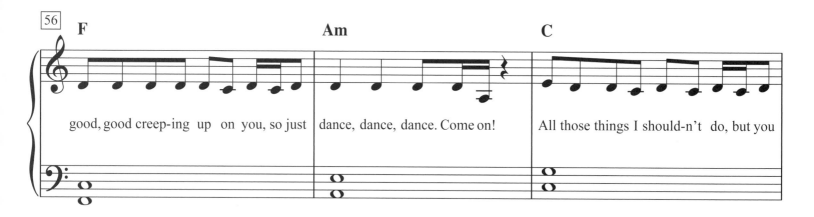

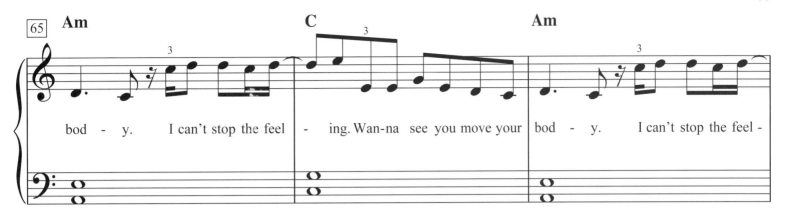

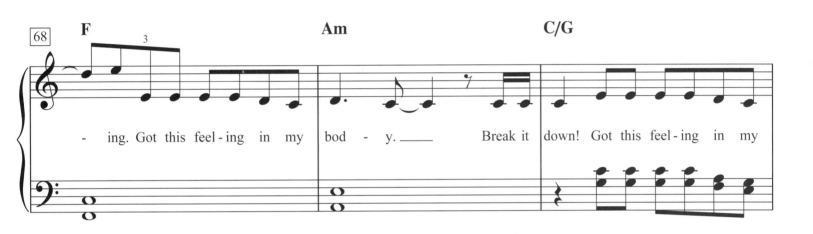

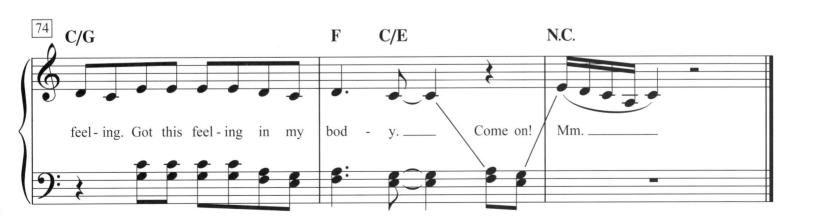

Firework

Words and Music by KATY PERRY,
MIKKEL ERIKSEN, TOR ERIK HERMANSEN,
ESTHER DEAN and SANDY WILHELM

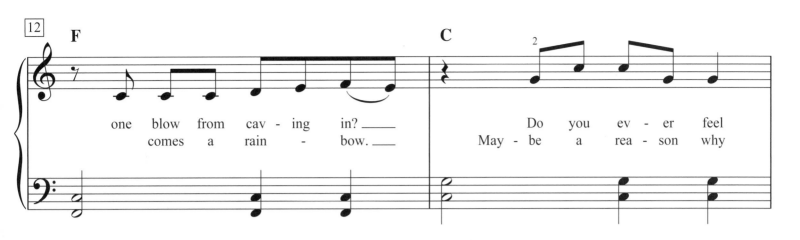

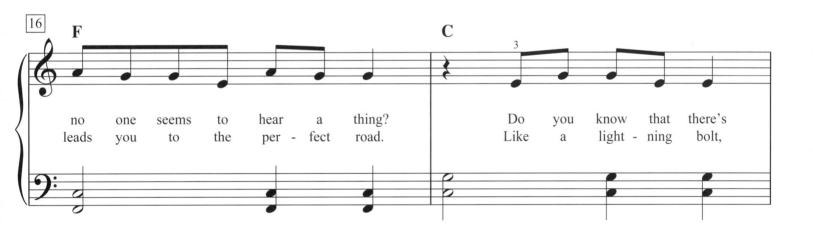

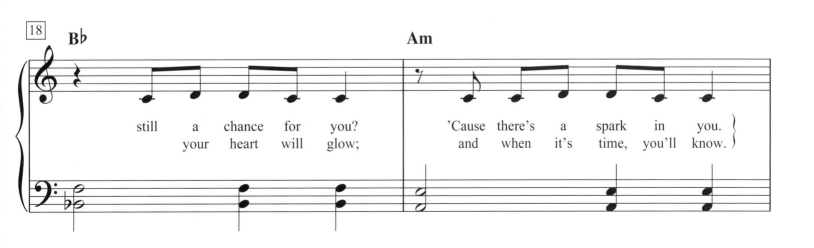

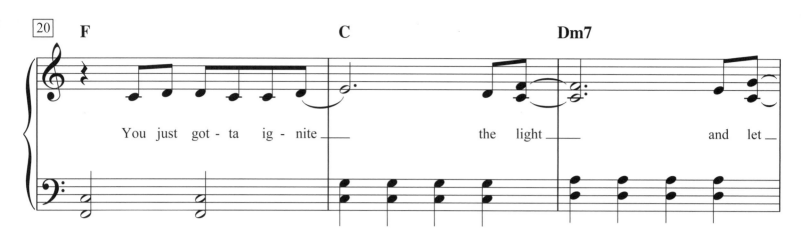

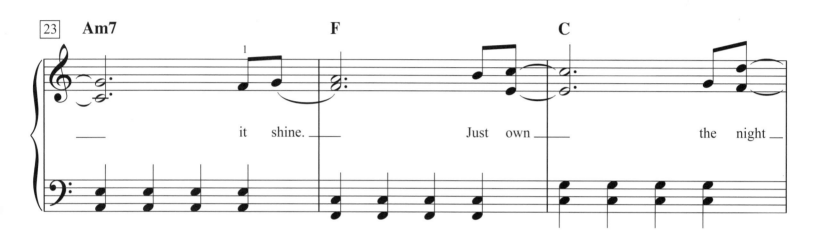

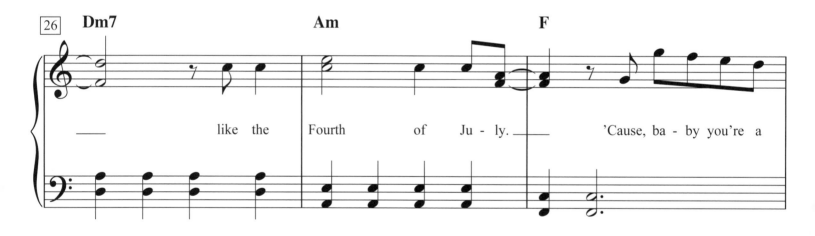

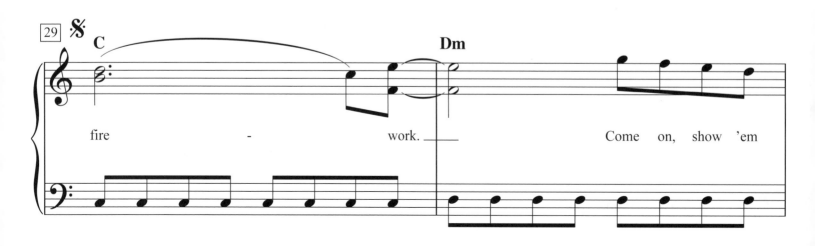

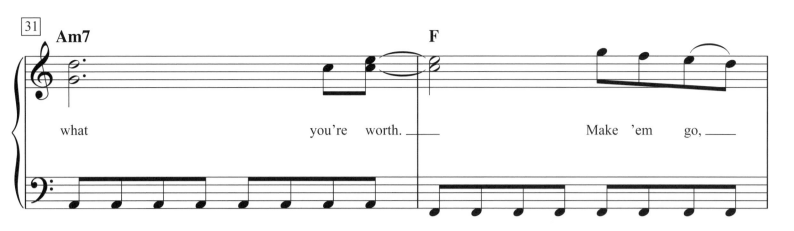

what you're worth. ___ Make 'em go, ___

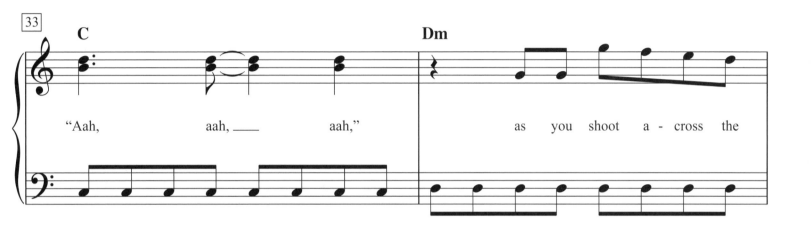

"Aah, aah, ___ aah," as you shoot a - cross the

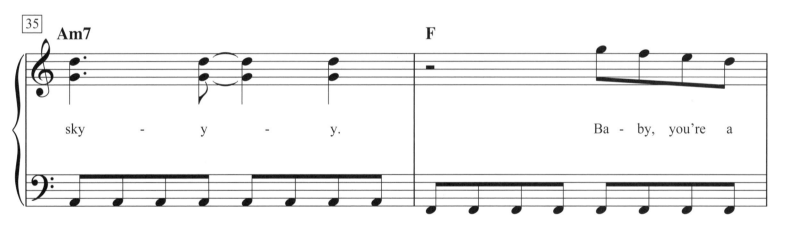

sky - y - y. Ba - by, you're a

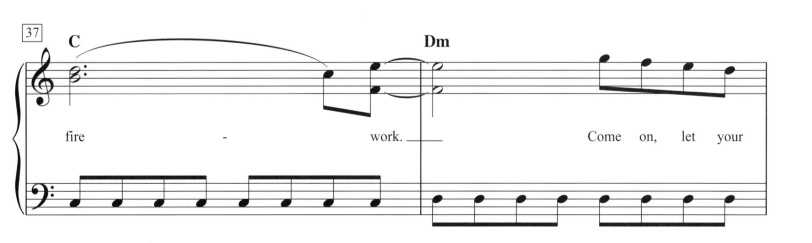

fire - work. ___ Come on, let your

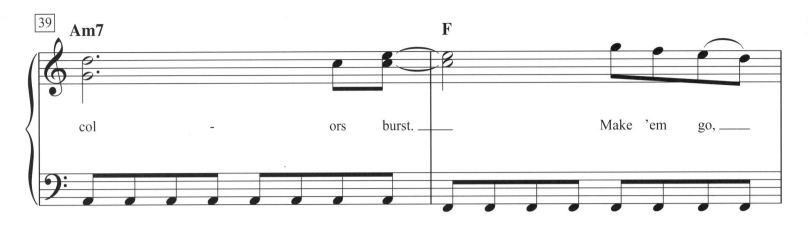

col - ors burst. ___ Make 'em go, ___

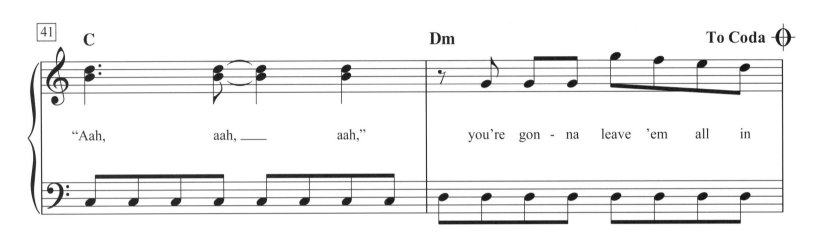

"Aah, aah, ___ aah," you're gon - na leave 'em all in

awe, awe, ___ awe. ___

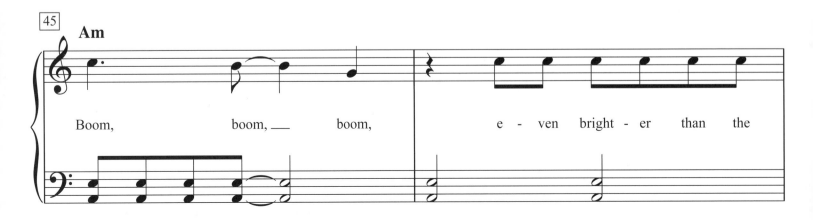

Boom, boom, ___ boom, e - ven bright - er than the

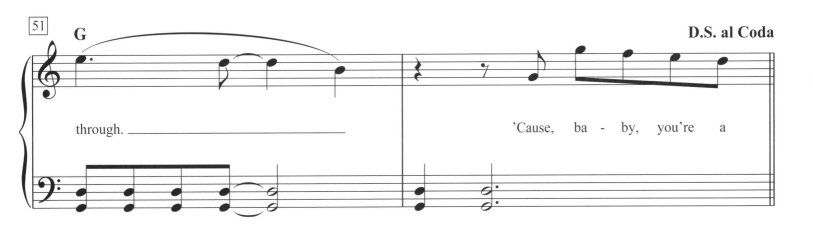

48

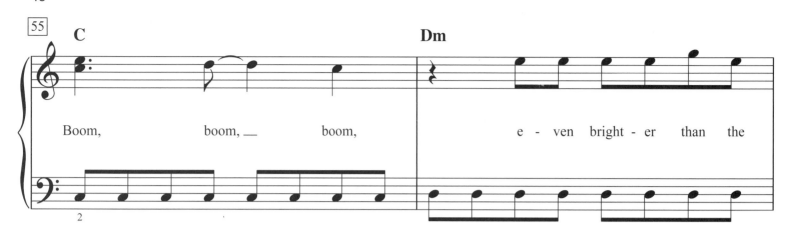

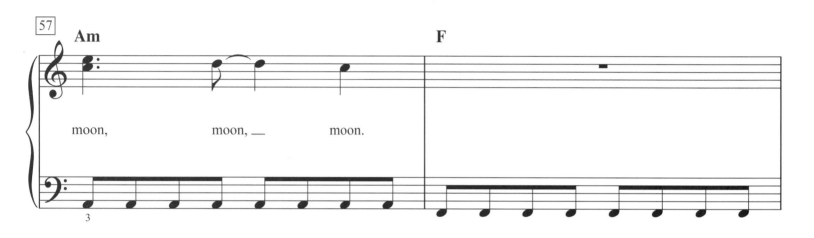

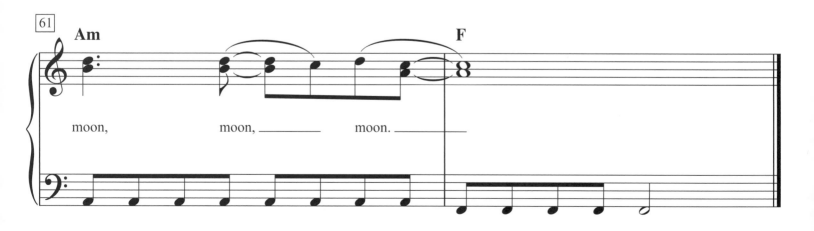

Lead the Way

from RAYA AND THE LAST DRAGON

Music and Lyrics by
JHENÉ AIKO

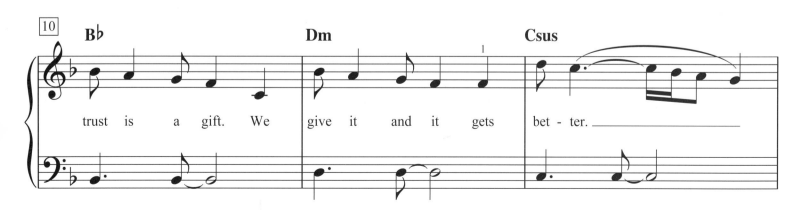

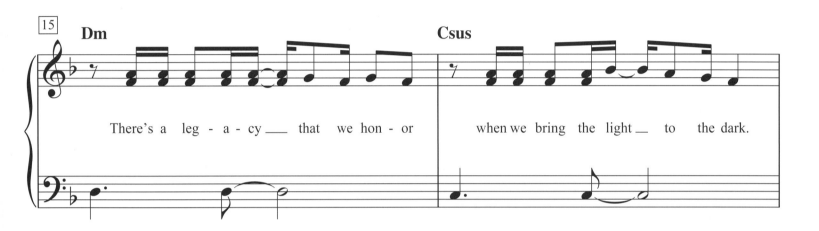

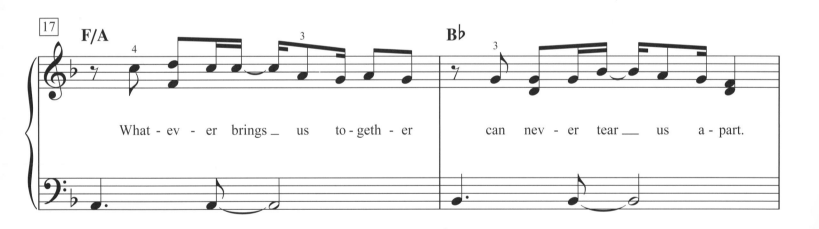

51

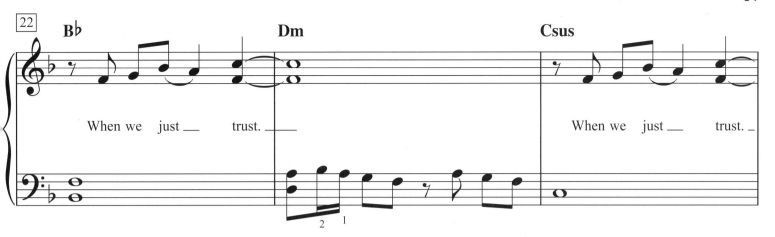

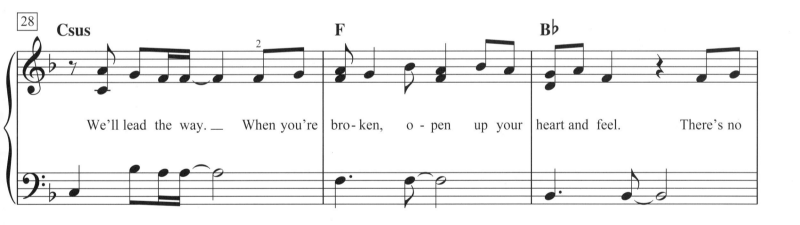

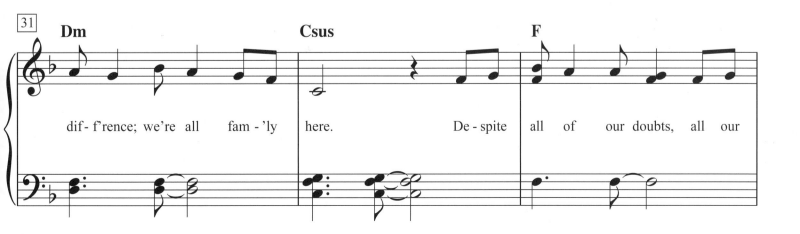

52

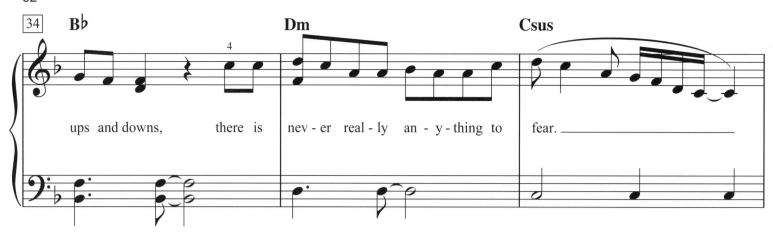

ups and downs, there is nev-er real-ly an-y-thing to fear. _____

There's an en-er-gy ___ in the wa-ter. There is mag-ic deep ___ in our heart.

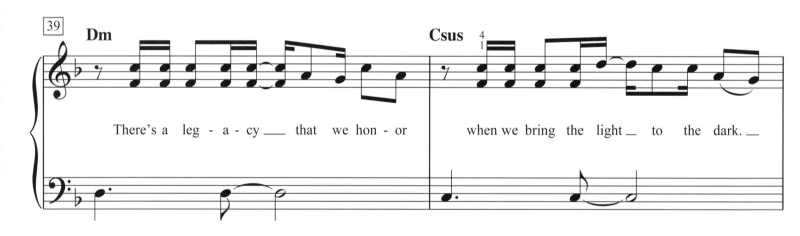

There's a leg-a-cy ___ that we hon-or when we bring the light ___ to the dark. ___

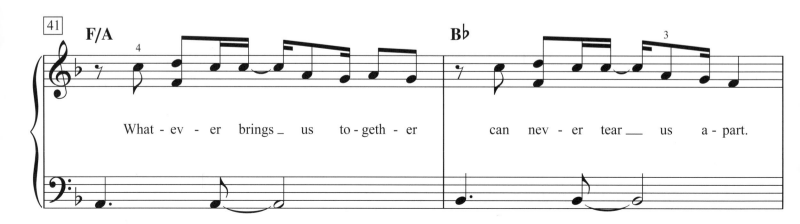

What-ev-er brings ___ us to-geth-er can nev-er tear ___ us a-part.

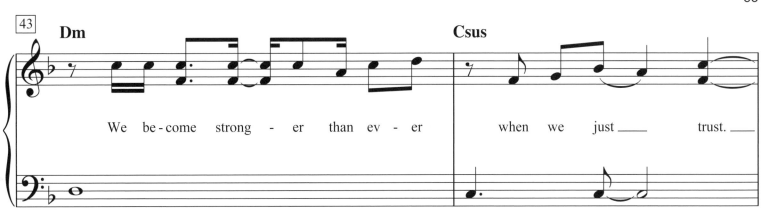

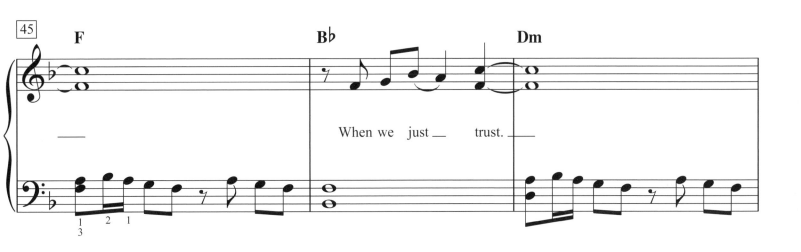

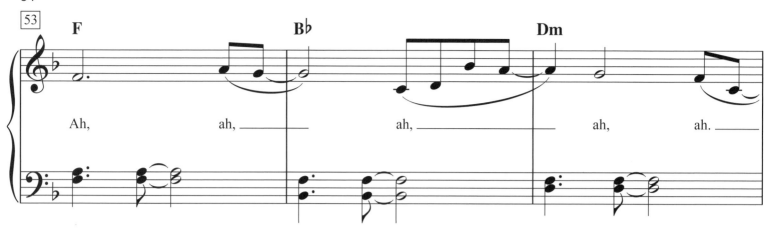

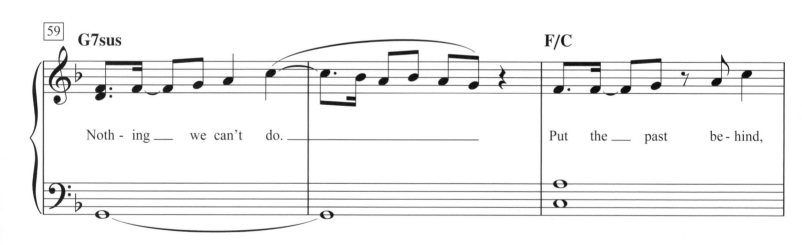

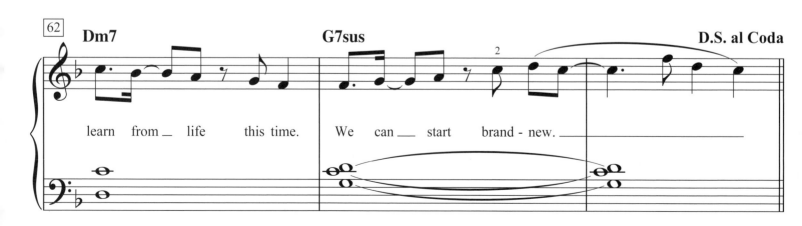

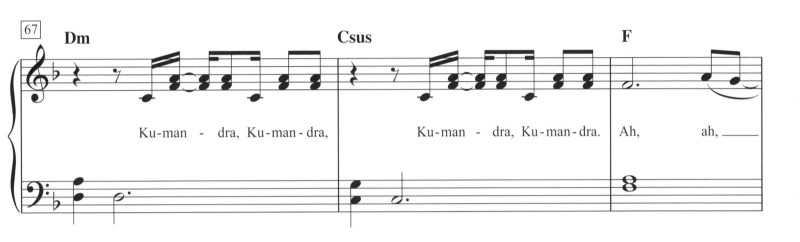

Happy

from DESPICABLE ME 2

Words and Music by
PHARRELL WILLIAMS

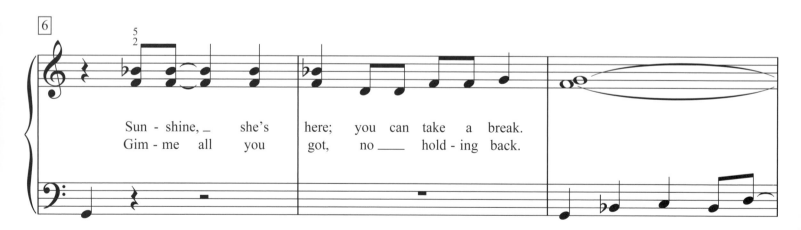

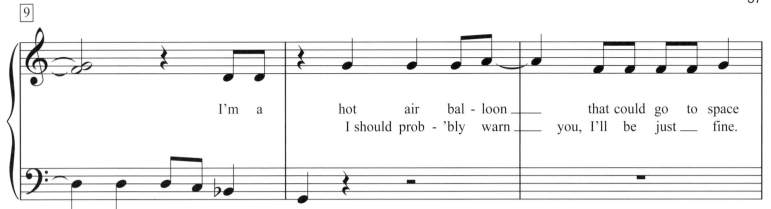

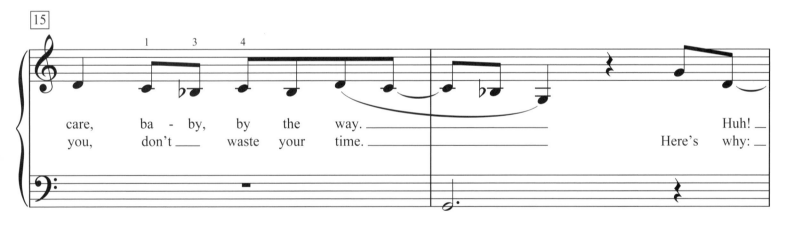

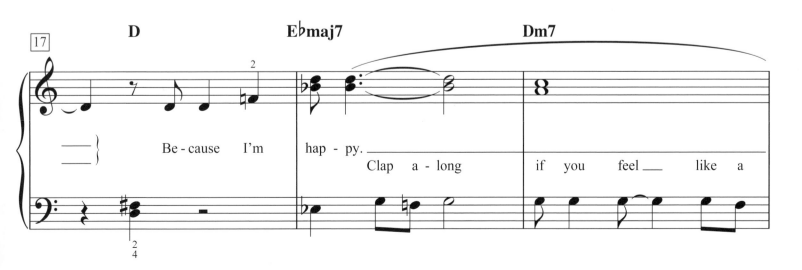

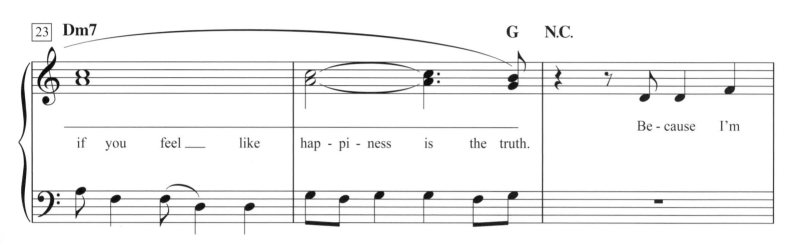

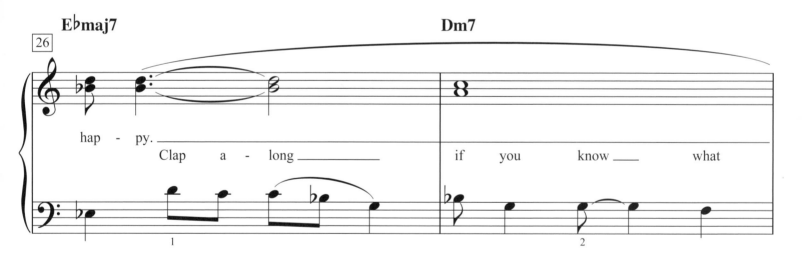

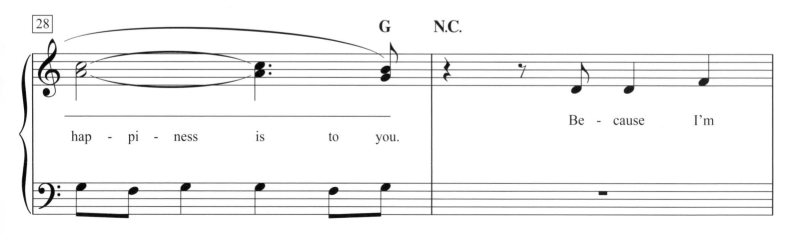

60

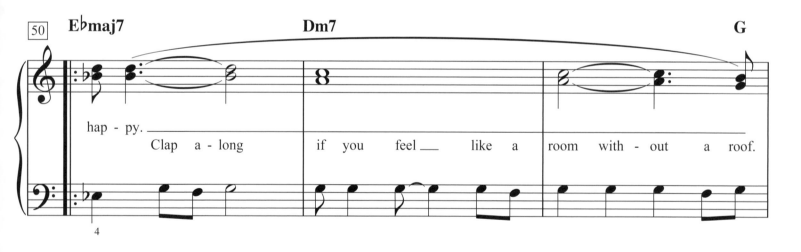

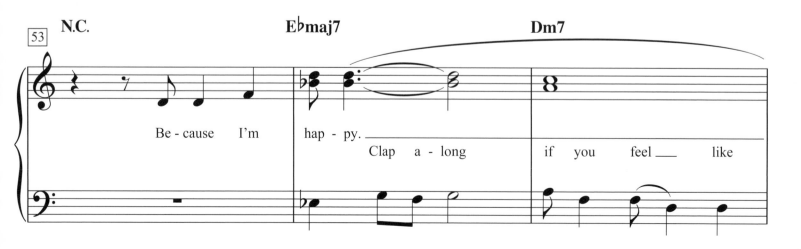

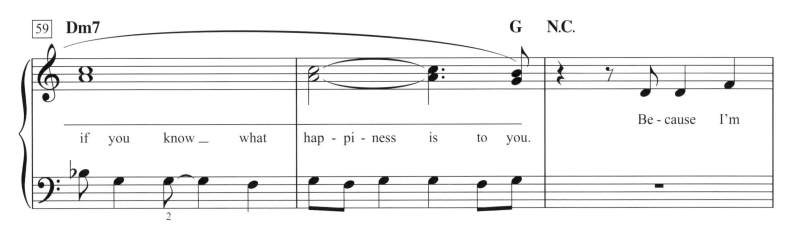

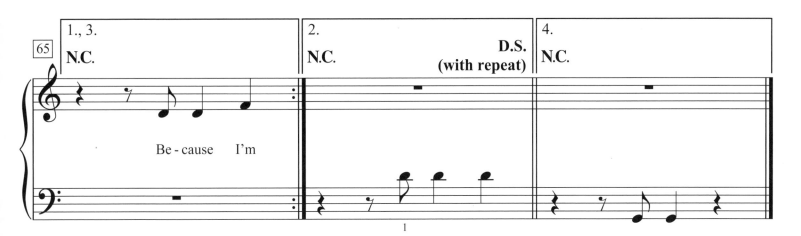

I Love

Words and Music by
TOM T. HALL

I love little baby ducks,
I love leaves __ in the wind,
I love o - pen hon - est smiles,

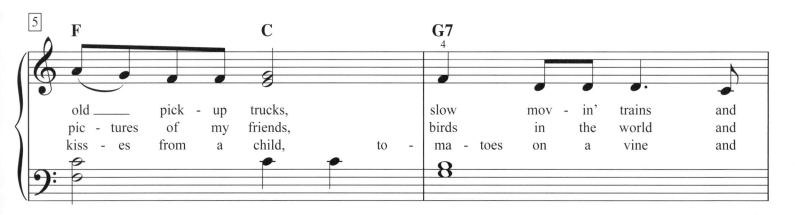

old __ pick - up trucks,
pic - tures of my friends,
kiss - es from a child, to -

slow mov - in' trains and
birds in the world and
ma - toes on a vine and

rain.
squirrels.
onions.

I love
I love
I love

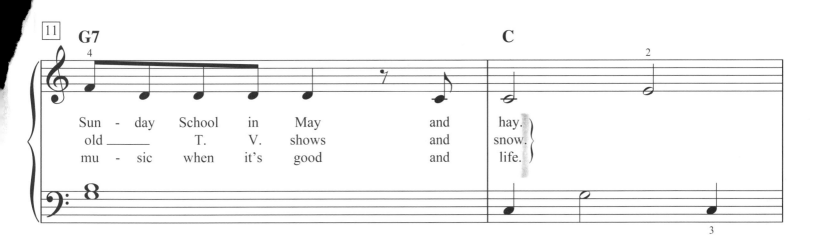

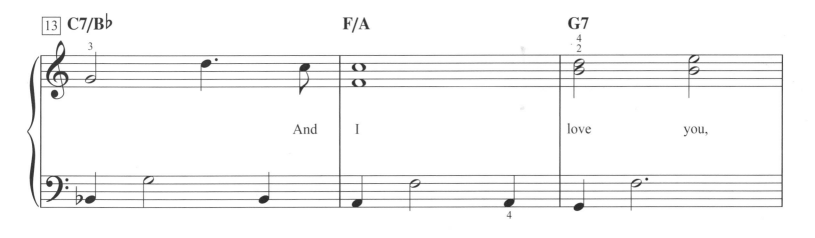

Mah-Nà Mah-Nà

By PIERO

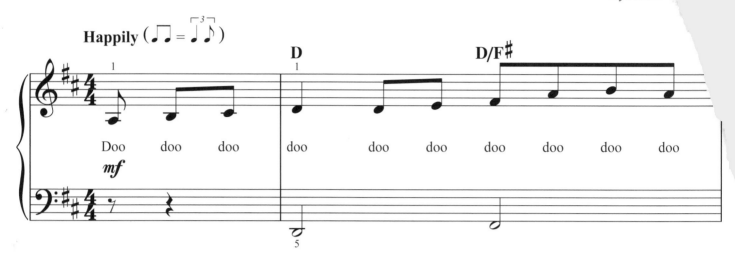

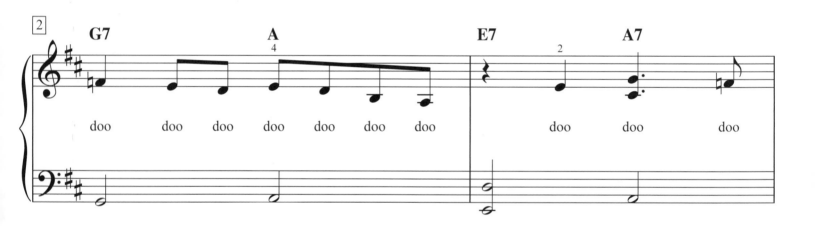

65

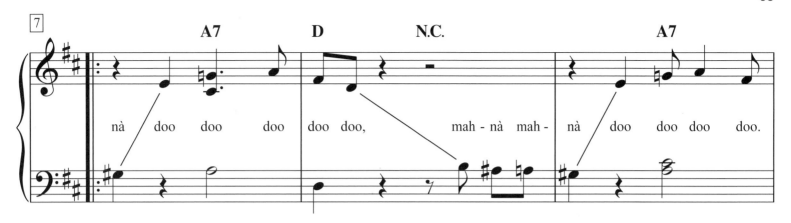

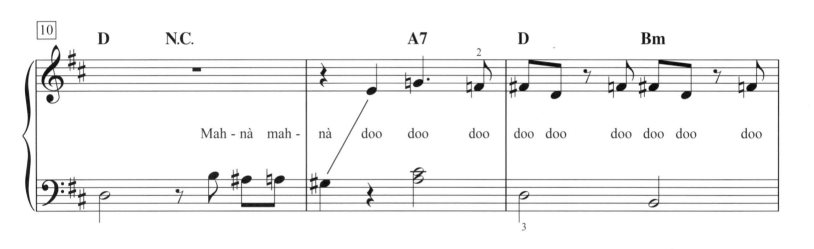

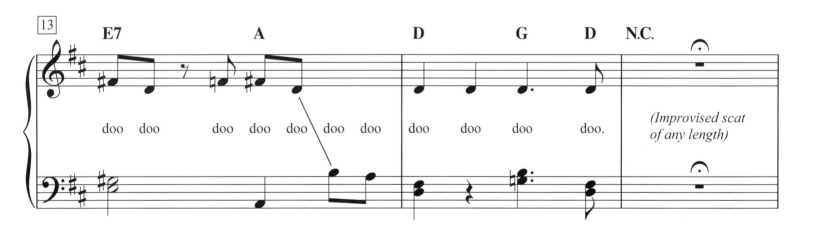

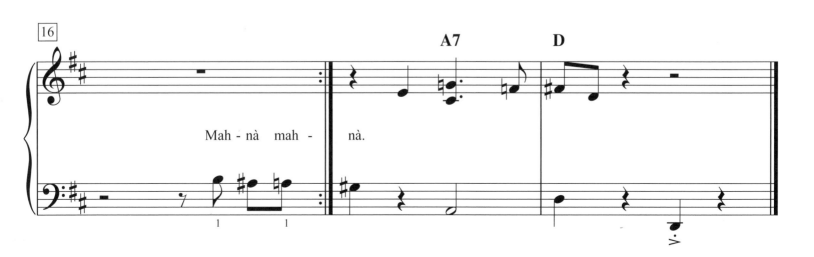

Pollywog in a Bog

Words and Music by JAMES CREEGGAN
and ED ROBERTSON

In a pud-dle by the trail, flips his ti-ny tail,

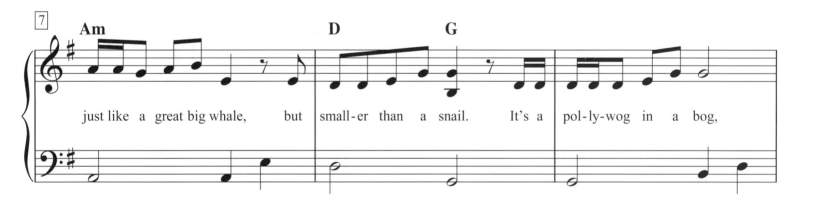

just like a great big whale, but small-er than a snail. It's a pol-ly-wog in a bog,

swims un-der sog-gy logs, one day he'll be a frog, pol-ly-wog in a bog. Oh oh oh

oh oh oh. ___   Oh, oh oh. ___   Oh, _____

oh, oh - ho. ___   O - ver - head a ce - dar tree   gives the shade he needs

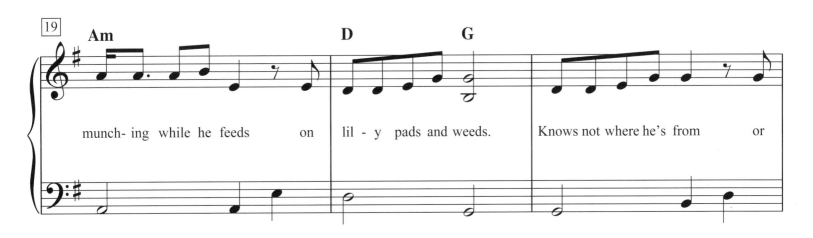

munch- ing while he feeds   on lil - y pads and weeds.   Knows not where he's from   or

how his life had be - gun.   He's not the on - ly one,   soon he'll breathe __ through

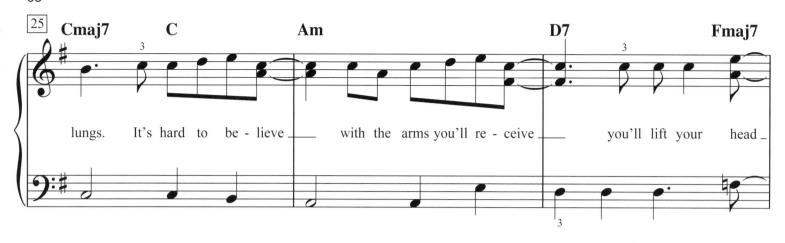

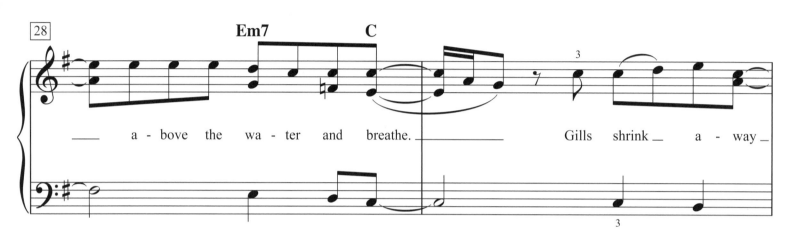

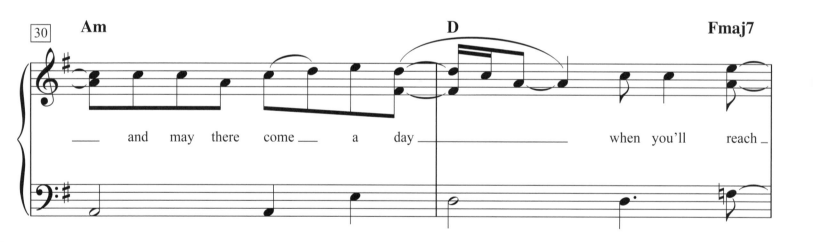

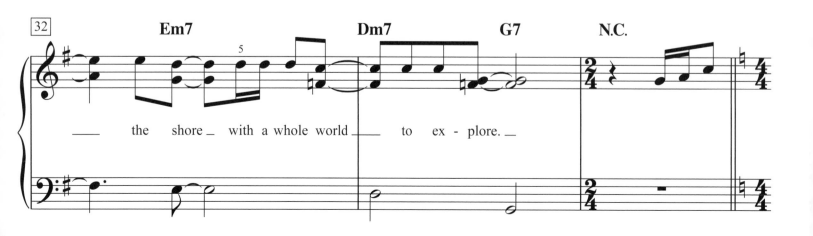

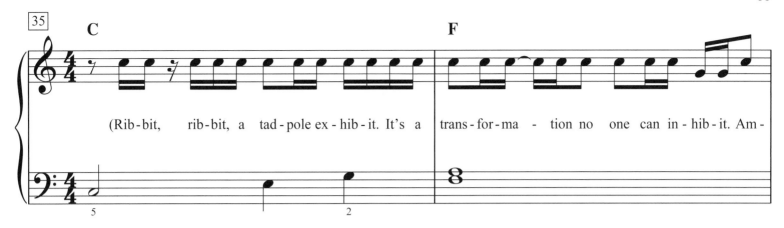

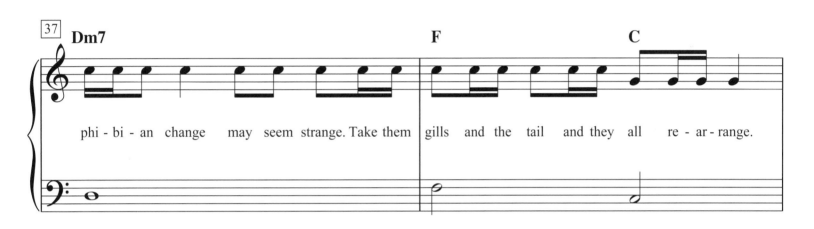

70

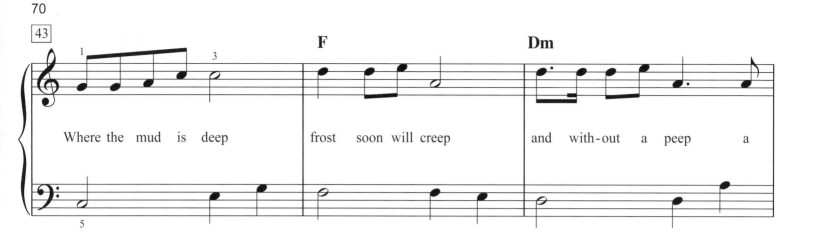

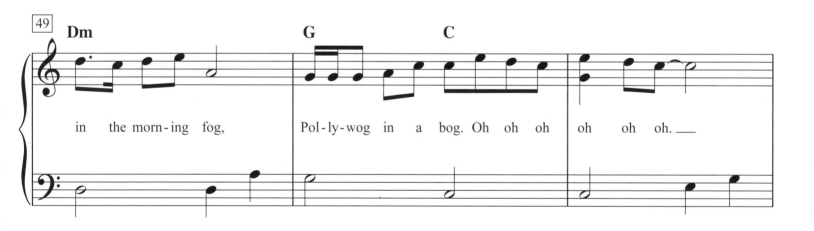

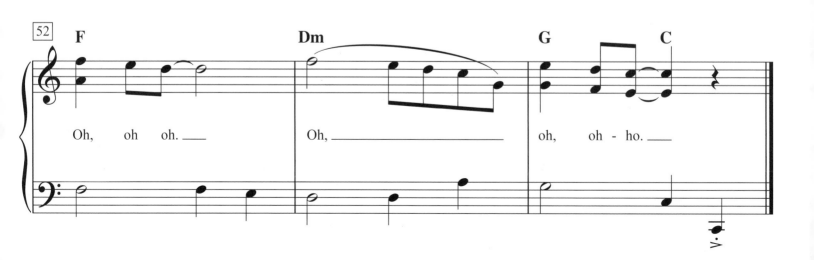

Me and Julio Down by the Schoolyard

Words and Music by
PAUL SIMON

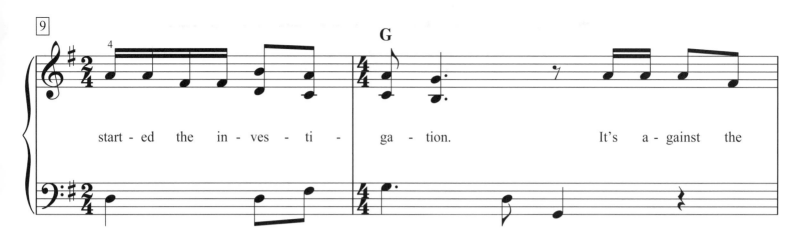

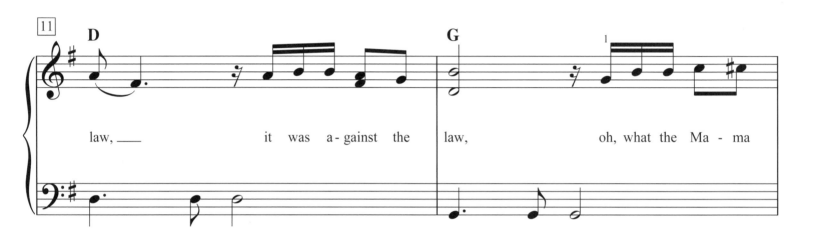

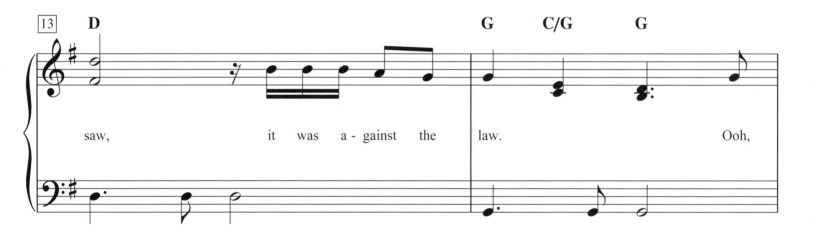

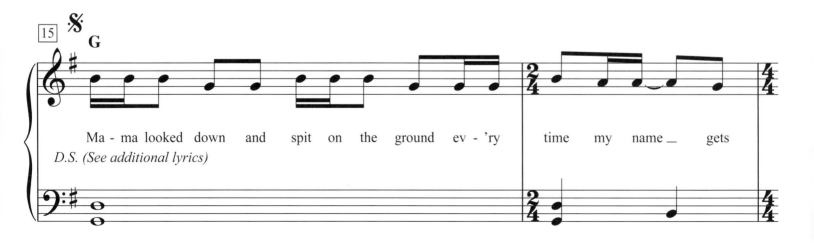

72

73

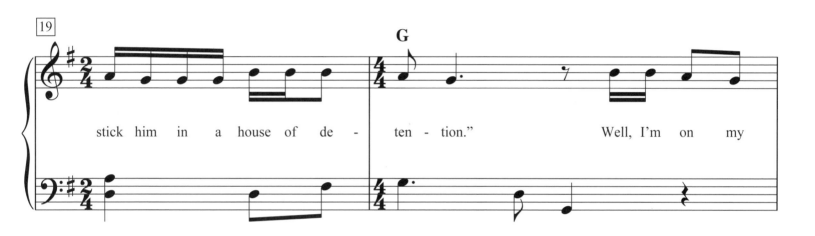

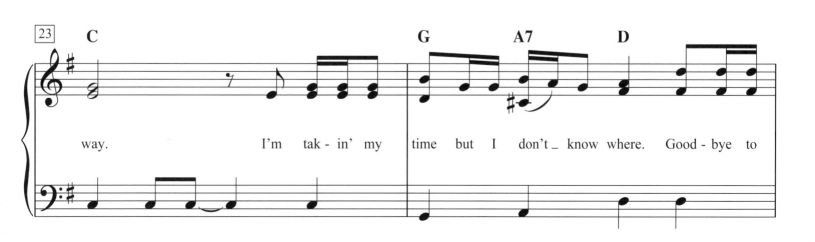

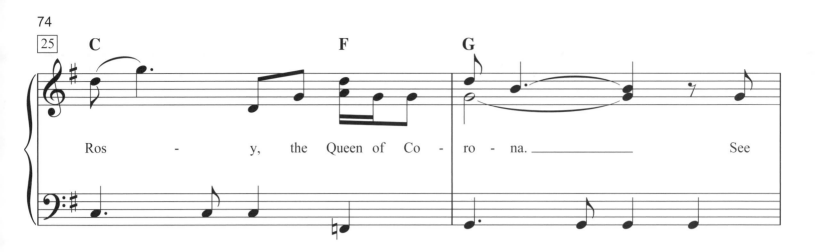

Ros - y, the Queen of Co - ro - na. _____ See

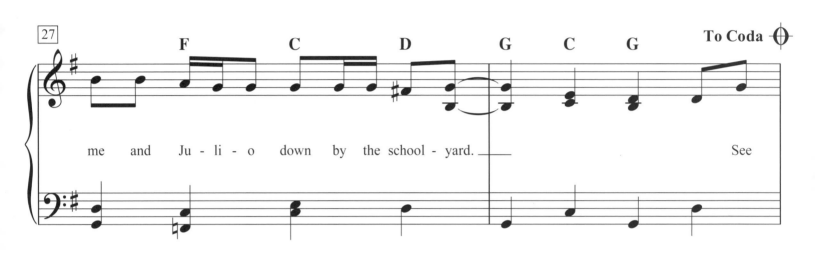

me and Ju - li - o down by the school - yard. ___ See

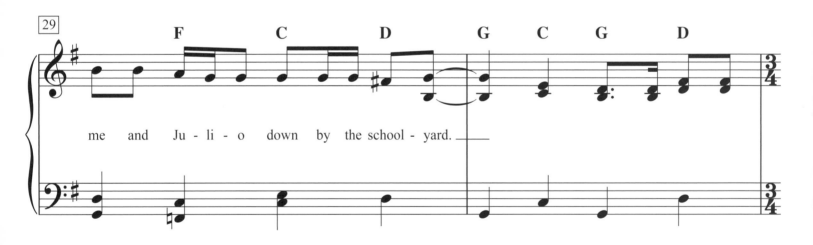

me and Ju - li - o down by the school - yard. ___

Whoa, __ in a

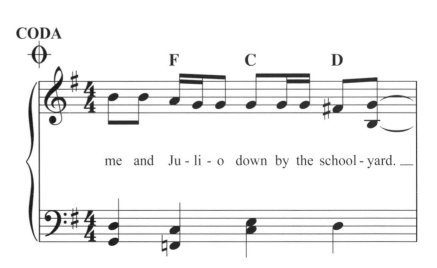

me and Ju - li - o down by the school - yard. __

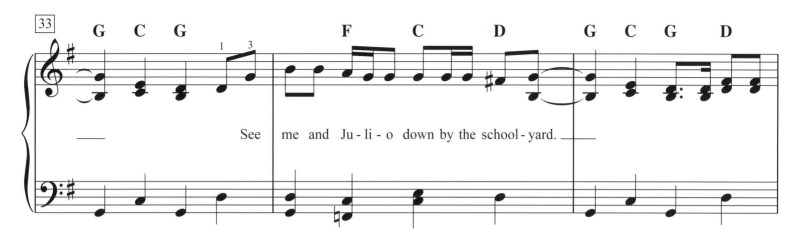

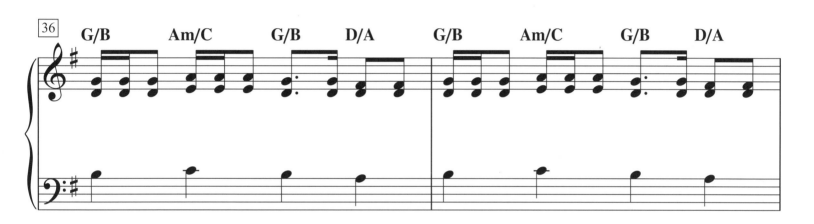

Additional Lyrics

In a couple of days they come and take me away
But the press let their story leak.
And when the radical Priest come to get me released
We was all on the cover of *Newsweek*.

Rescue

Words and Music by LAUREN DAIGLE,
JASON INGRAM and PAUL MABURY

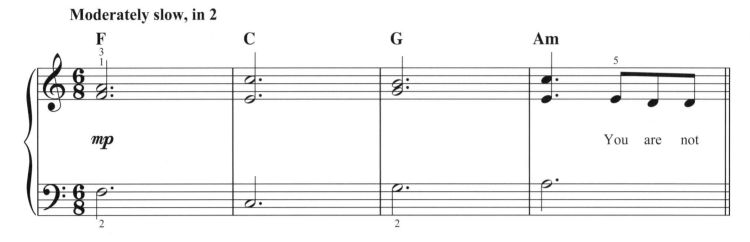

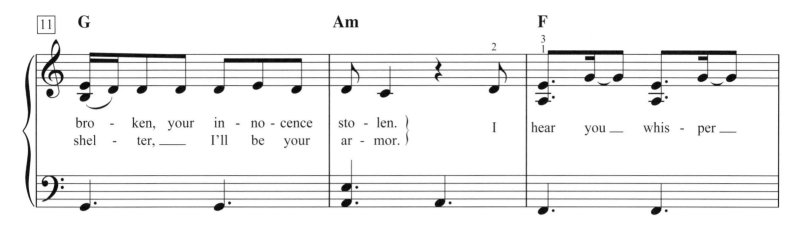

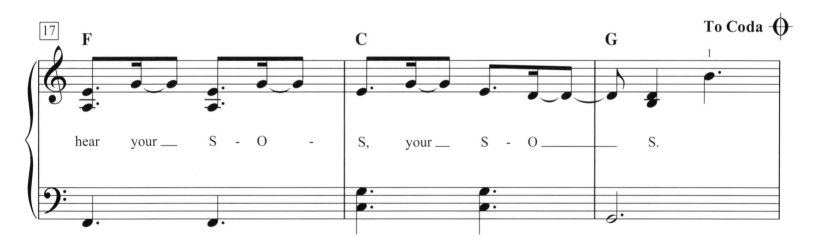

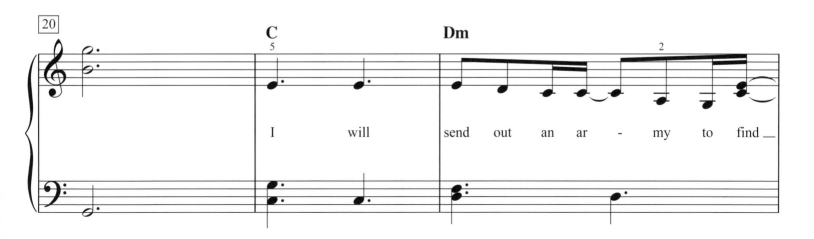

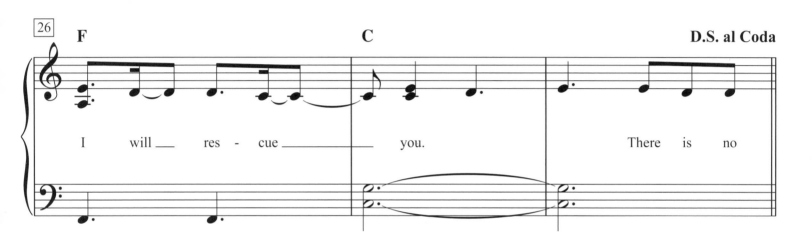

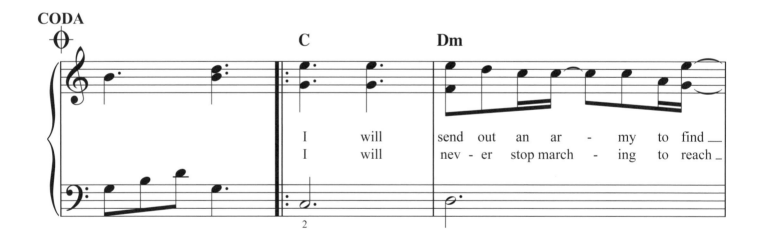

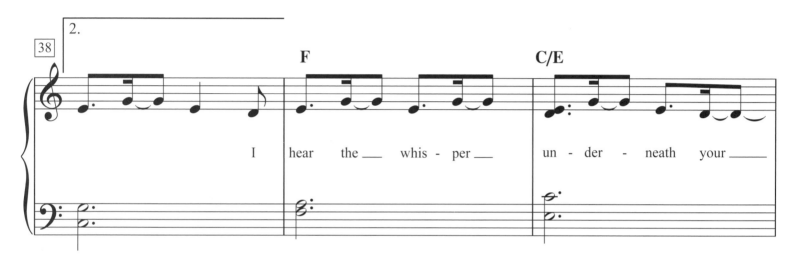

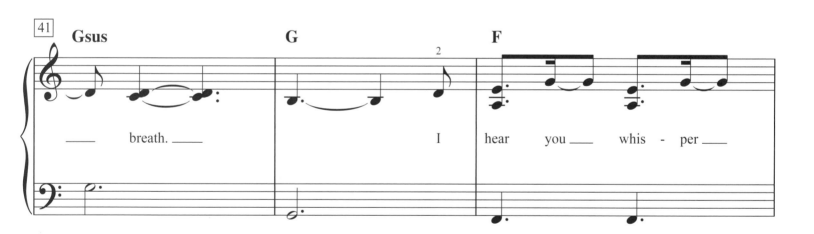

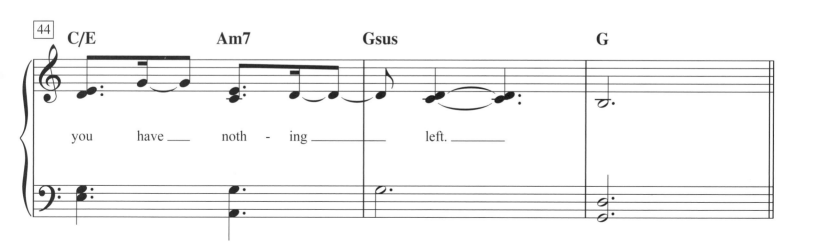

I   will   send out an ar - my to find_____   you   in the
I   will   nev - er stop march - ing to reach_____   you   in the

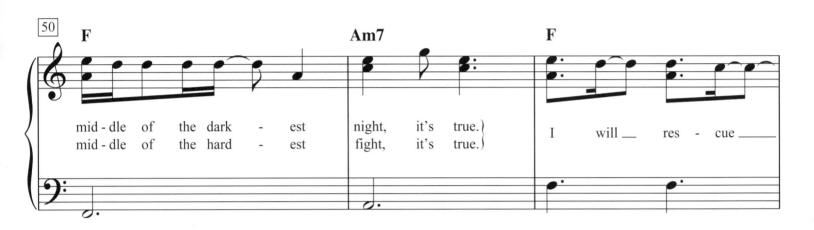

mid - dle   of   the   dark   -   est   night,   it's   true.)   I   will __   res - cue _____
mid - dle   of   the   hard   -   est   fight,   it's   true.)

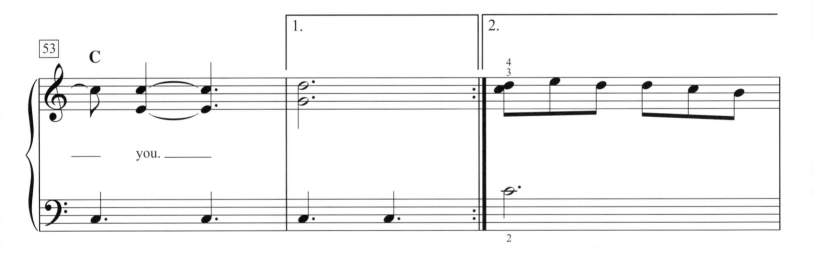

_____   you. _____

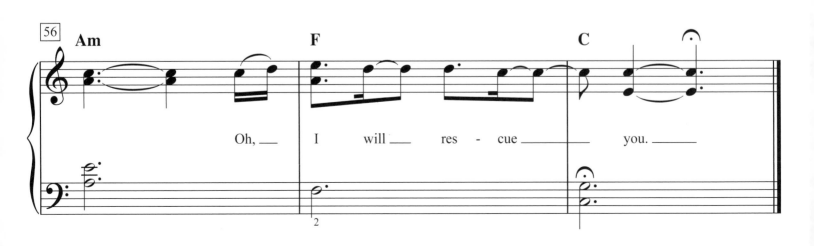

Oh, __   I   will __   res - cue _____   you. _____

Over the Rainbow

from THE WIZARD OF OZ

Music by HAROLD ARLEN
Lyric by E.Y. "YIP" HARBURG

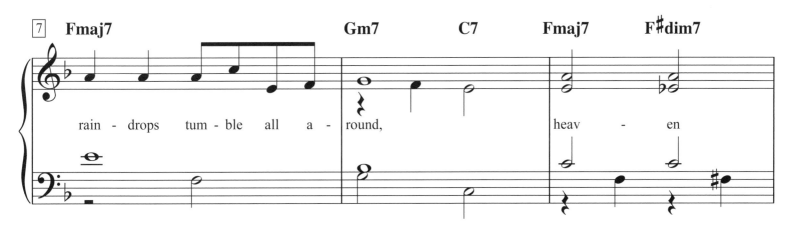

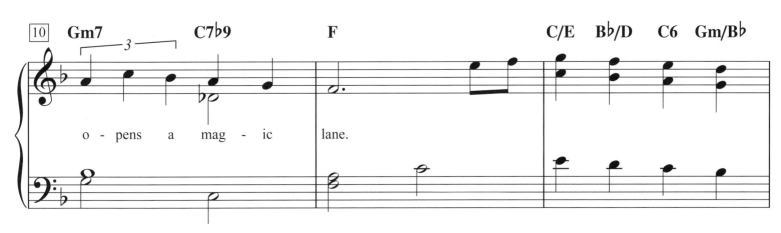

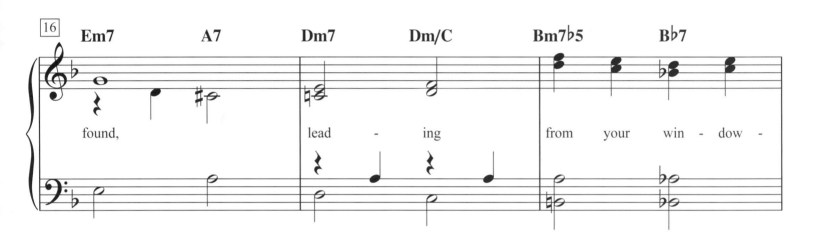

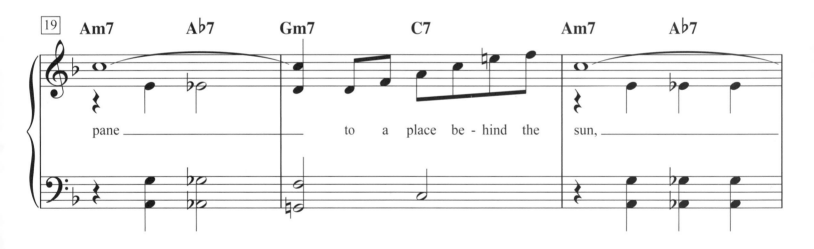

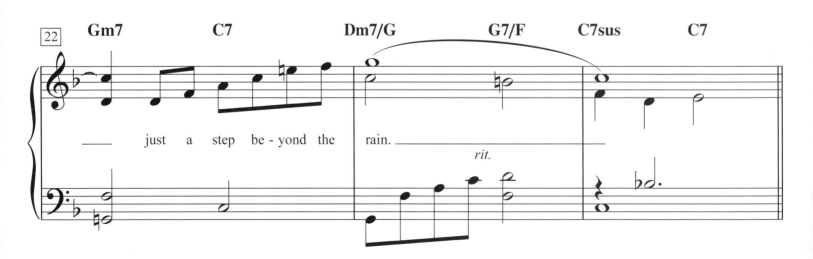

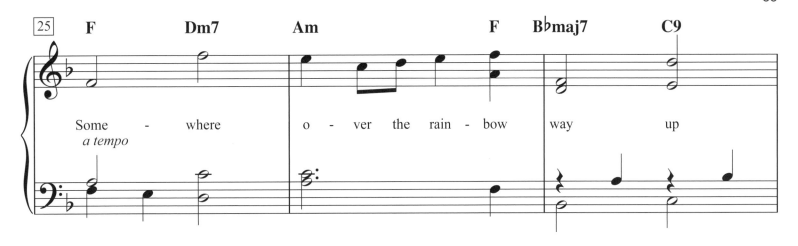

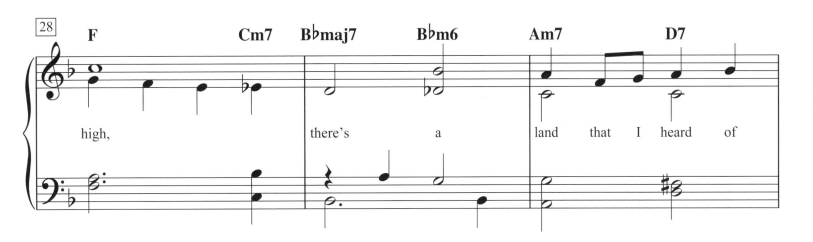

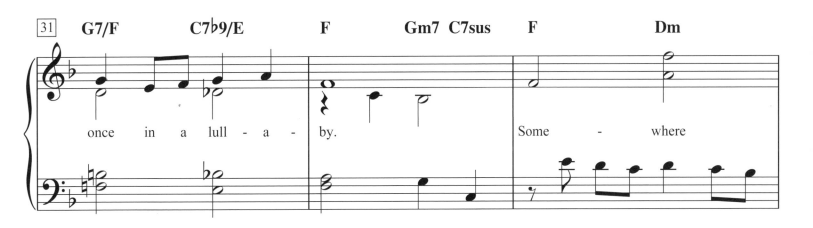

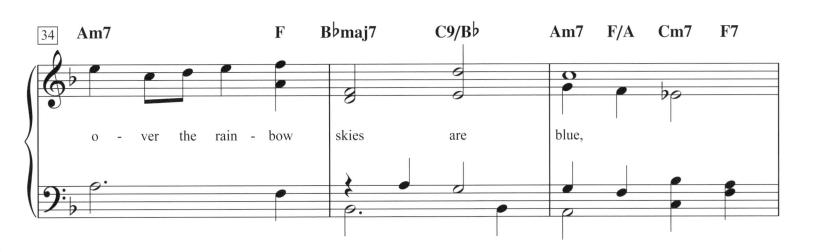

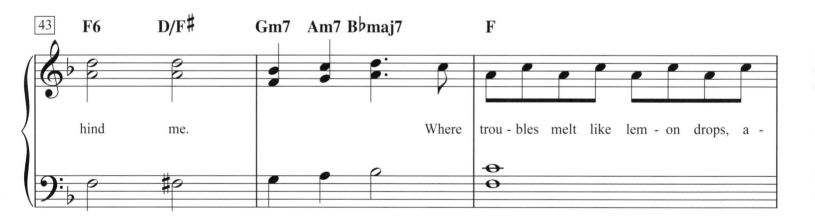

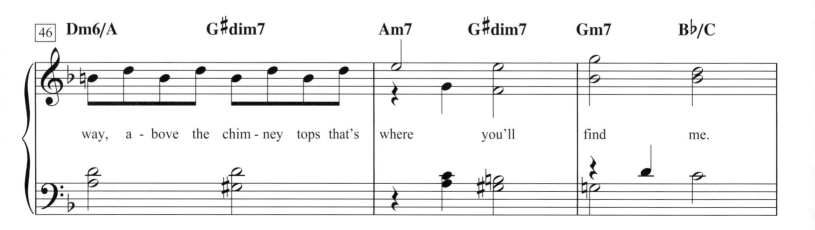

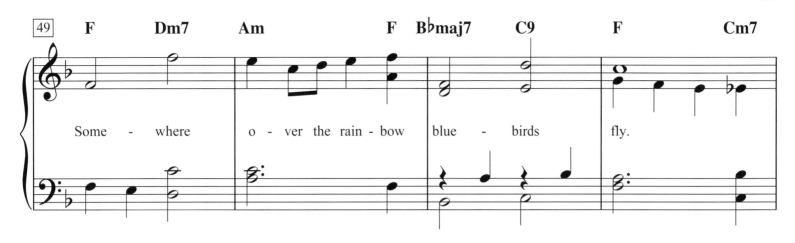

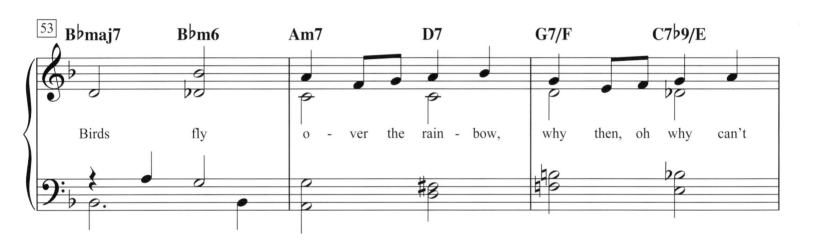

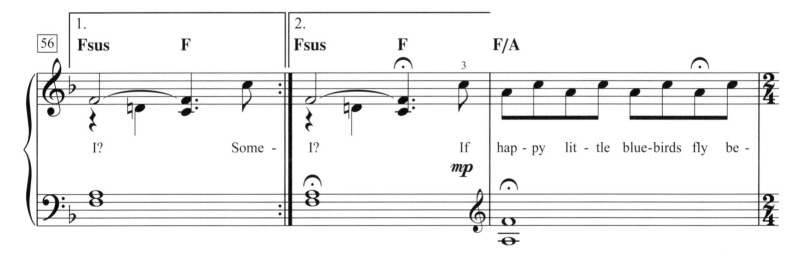

Remedy

Words and Music by ADELE ADKINS
and RYAN TEDDER

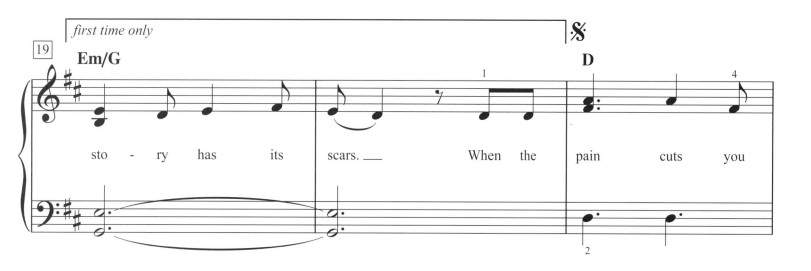

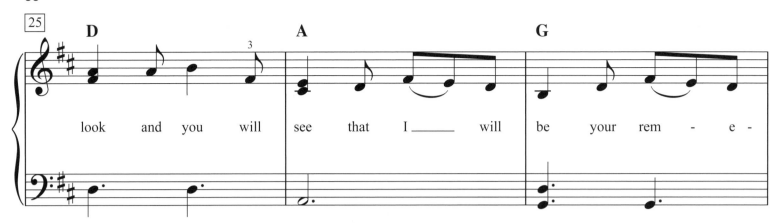

look and you will see that I _____ will be your rem - e -

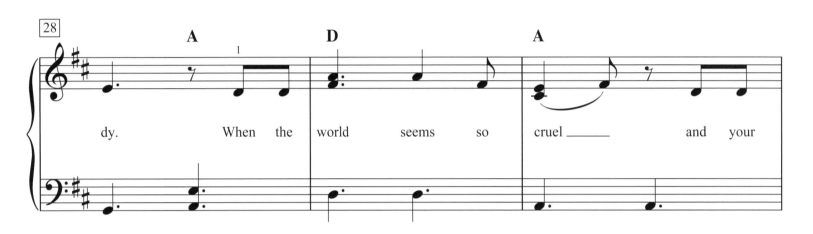

dy. When the world seems so cruel _____ and your

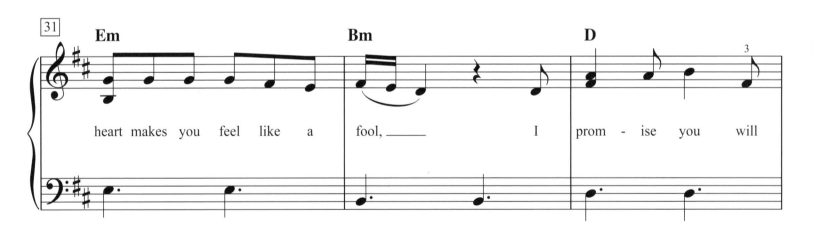

heart makes you feel like a fool, _____ I prom - ise you will

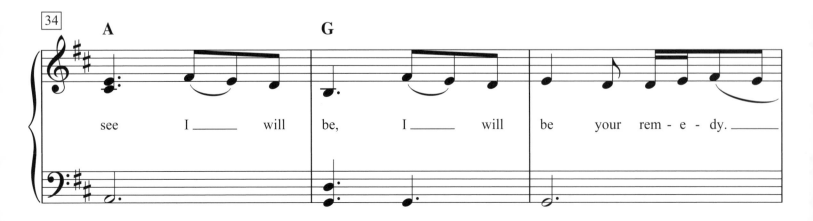

see I _____ will be, I _____ will be your rem - e - dy. _____

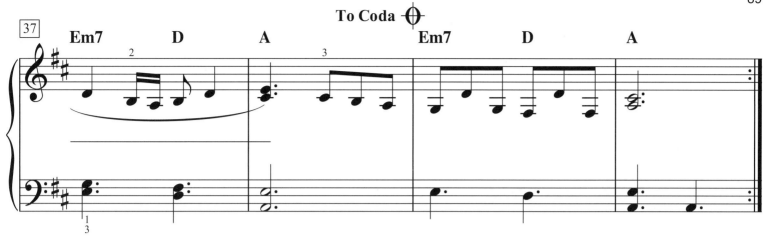

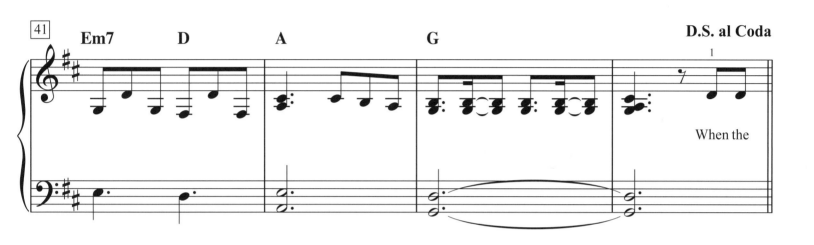

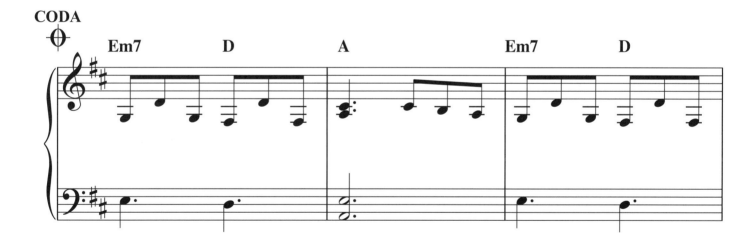

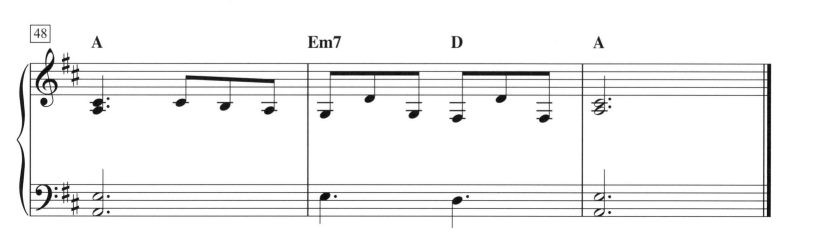

Theme from Spider Man

Written by BOB HARRIS
and PAUL FRANCIS WEBSTER

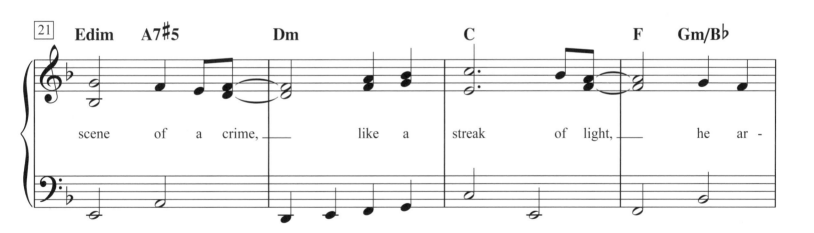

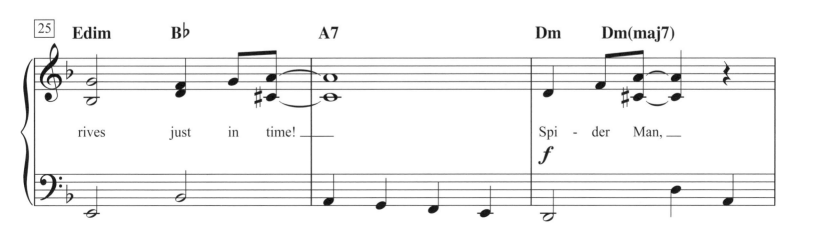

92

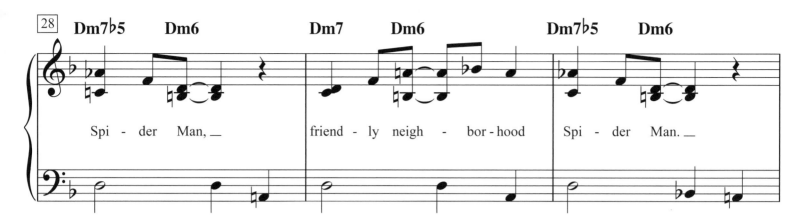

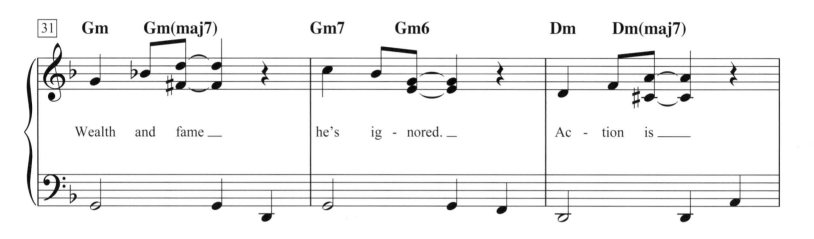

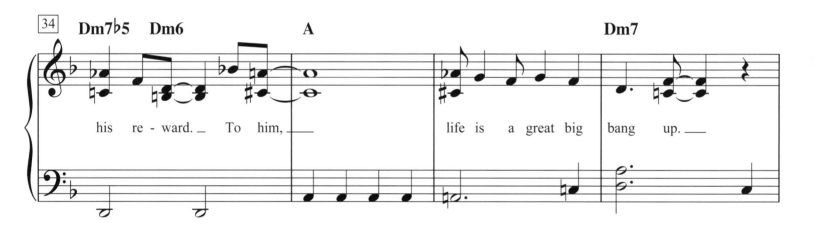

Respect

Words and Music by
OTIS REDDING

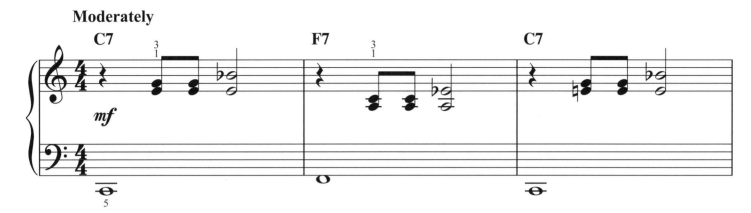

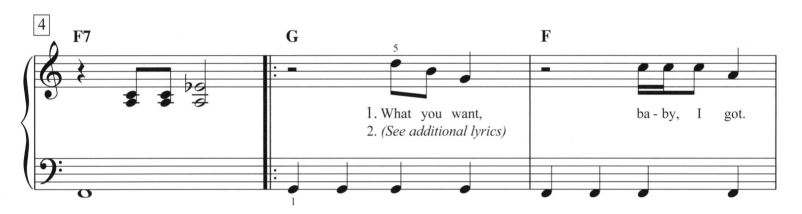

1. What you want,
2. (See additional lyrics)

ba - by, I got.

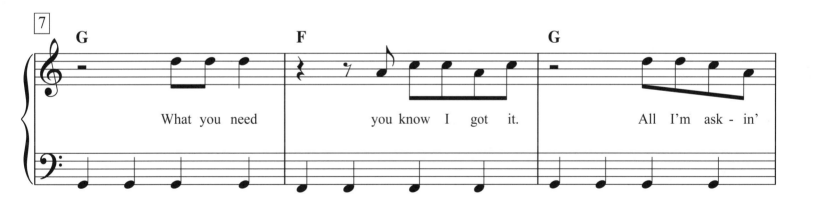

What you need

you know I got it.

All I'm ask - in'

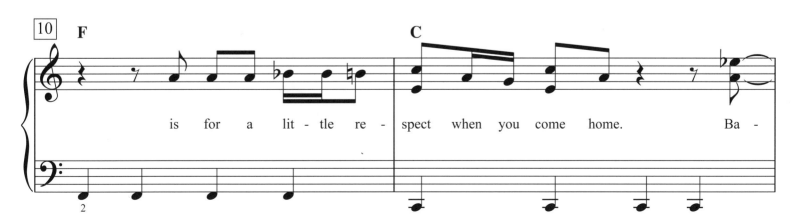

is for a lit - tle re - spect when you come home. Ba -

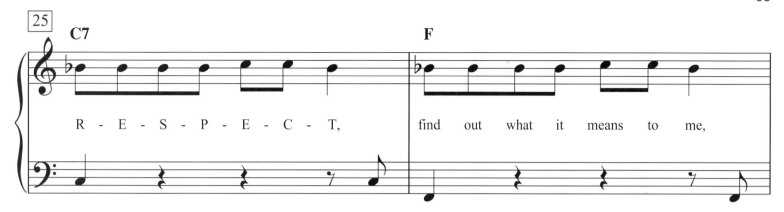

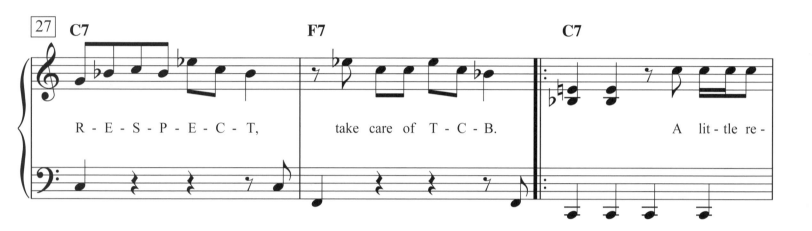

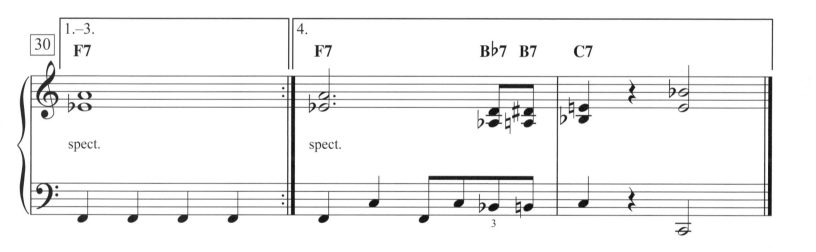

Additional Lyrics

2. I ain't gonna do you wrong while you gone.
   I ain't gonna do you wrong 'cause I don't wanna.
   All I'm askin' is for a little respect, when you come home.
   Baby, when you come home, respect.

4. Ooh, your kisses, sweeter than honey,
   And guess what, so here's my money,
   All I want you to do for me is give it to me when you get home.
   Yeah, baby, when you get home.

You'll Sing a Song and I'll Sing a Song

Words and Music by
ELLA JENKINS

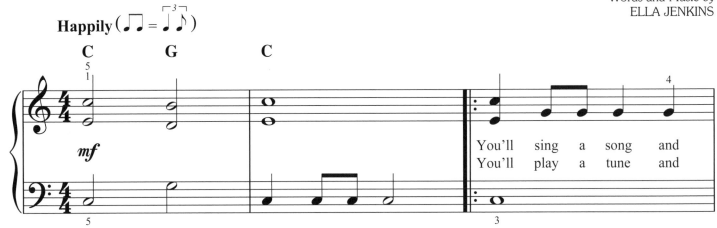

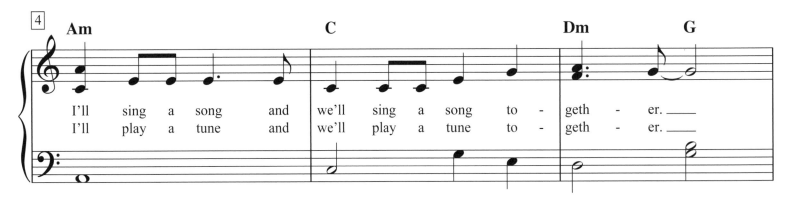

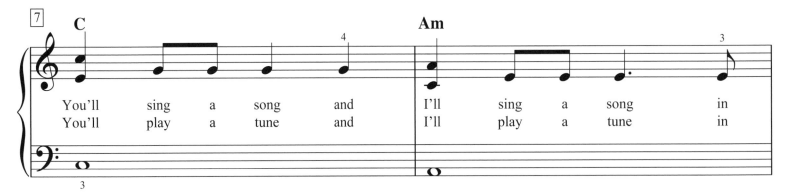

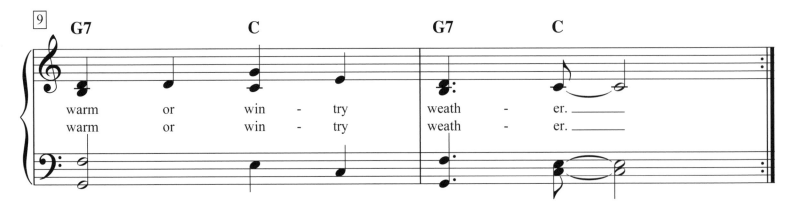

Additional Lyrics

3. You'll hum a line...
4. You'll whistle a tune...

This Is Me

from THE GREATEST SHOWMAN

Words and Music by BENJ PASEK
and JUSTIN PAUL

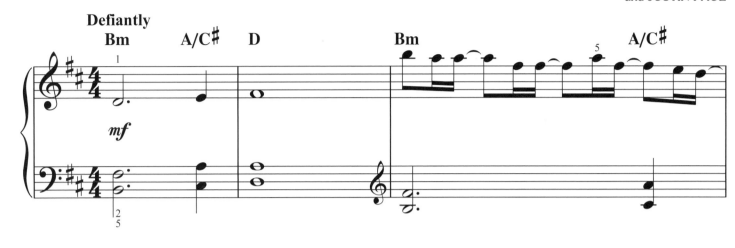

I am not a stran - ger to ___ the dark ___ Hide a - way, _

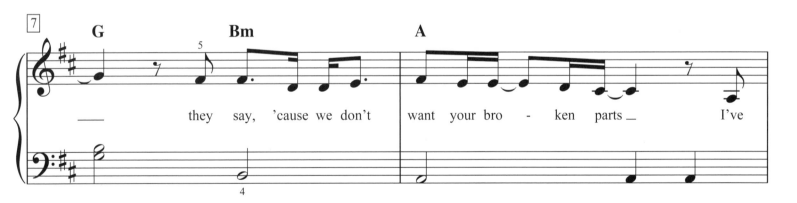

___ they say, 'cause we don't want your bro - ken parts ___ I've

learned _ to be __ a - shamed _ of all ___ my scars Run a - way, _

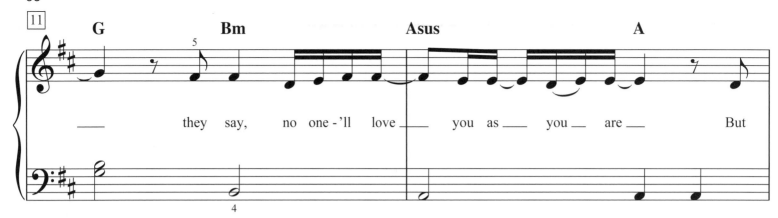

they say, no one -'ll love ___ you as ___ you ___ are ___ But

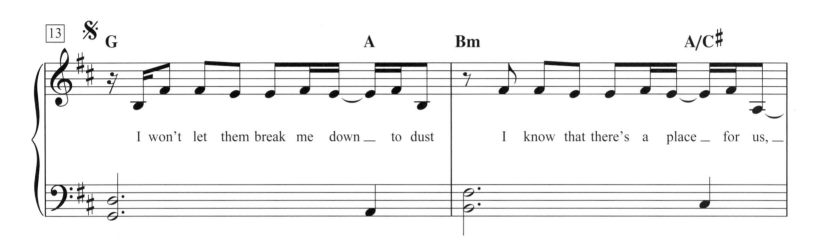

I won't let them break me down ___ to dust   I know that there's a place ___ for us, ___

___ for we are glo - ri - ous   When the

sharp - est words ___ wan - na cut me down ___ I'm gon - na

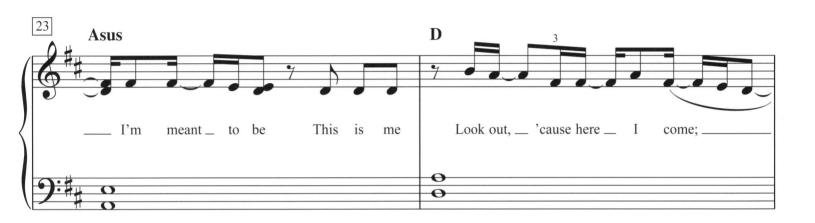

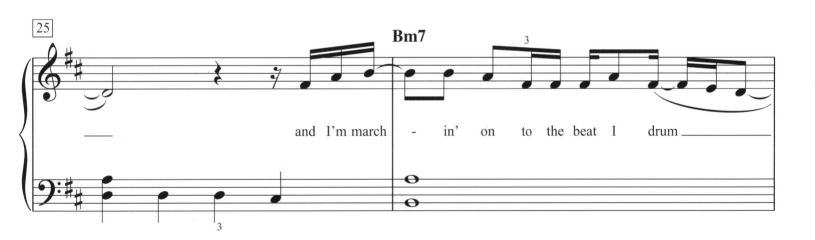

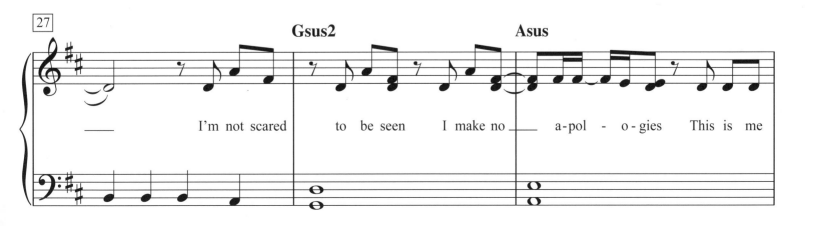

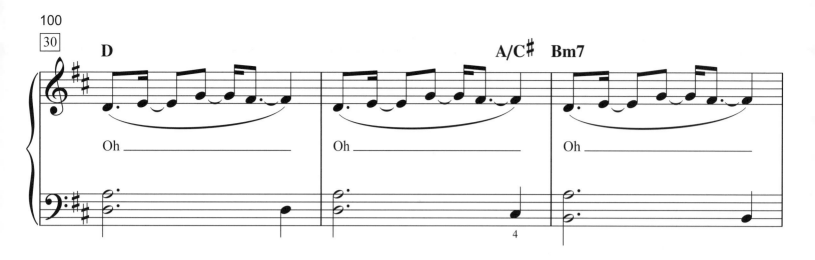

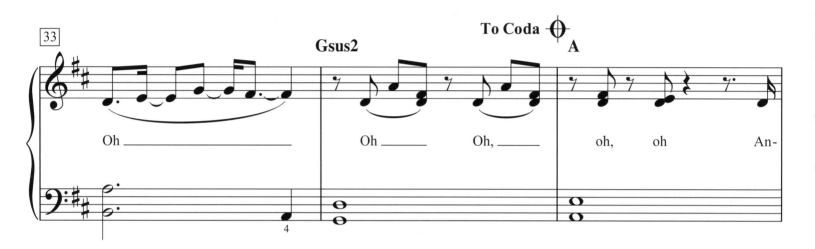

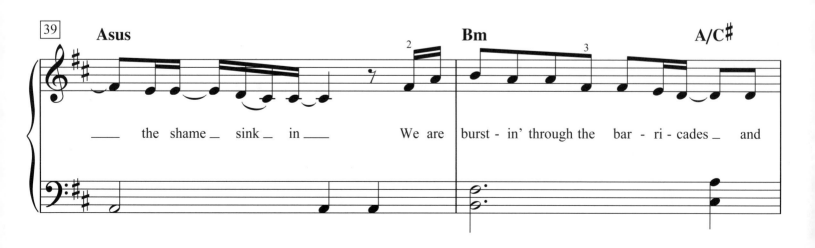

D.S. al Coda

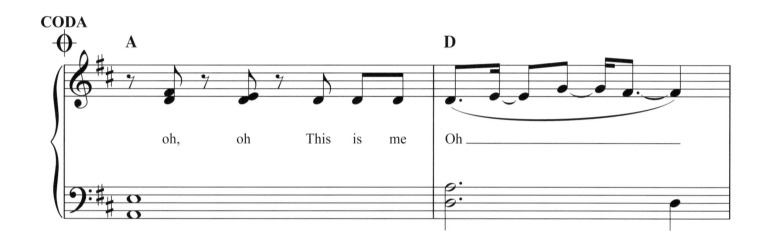

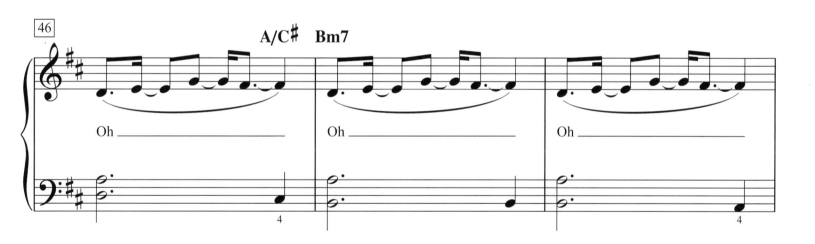

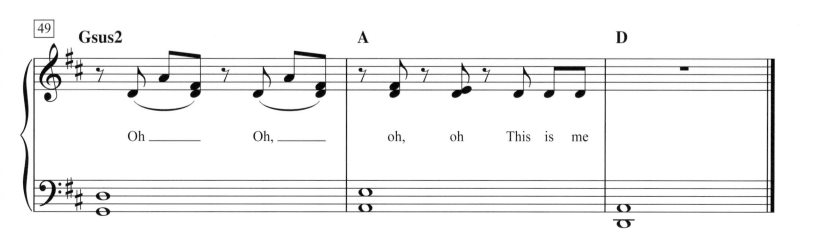

Wake Me Up!

Words and Music by ALOE BLACC,
TIM BERGLING and MICHAEL EINZIGER

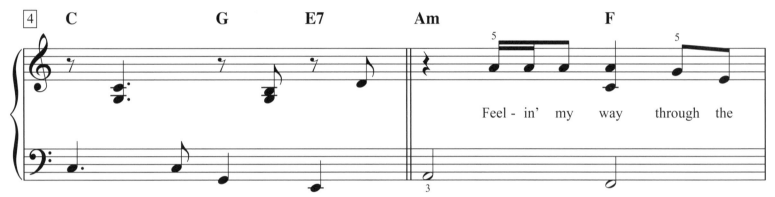

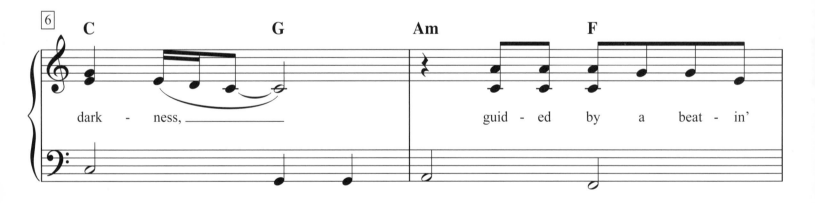

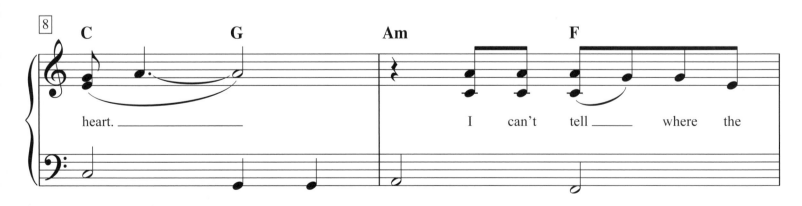

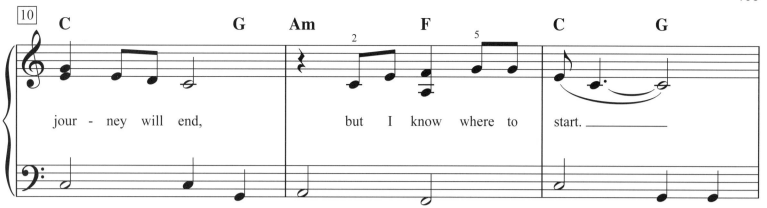

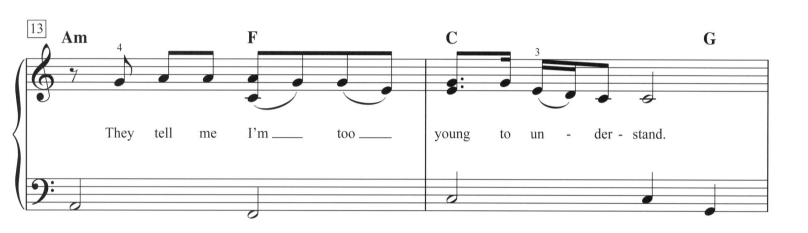

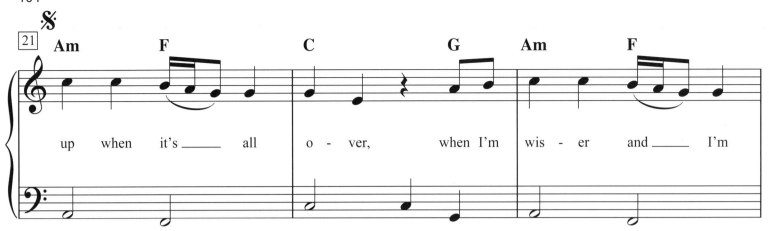

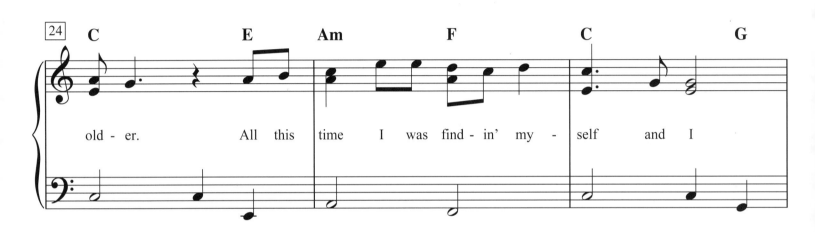

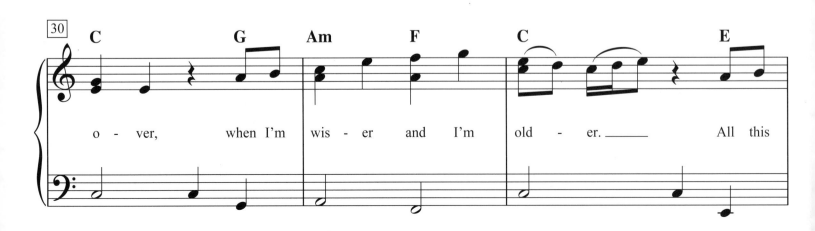

time I was find-in' my - self_____ and I_____ did-n't know I was

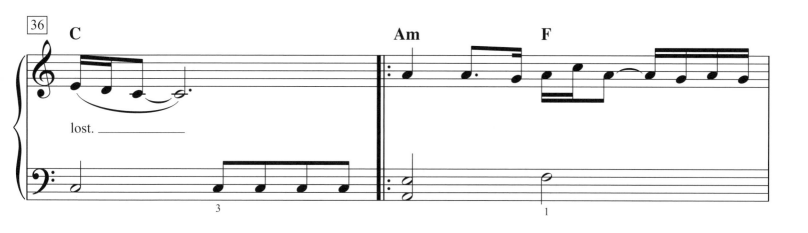

lost._____

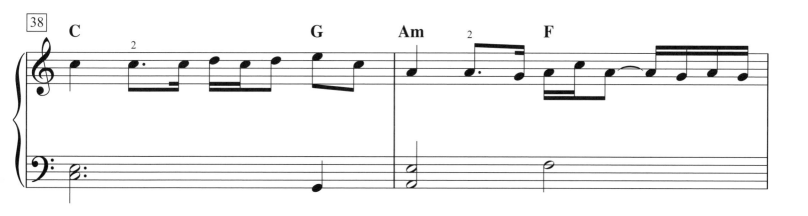

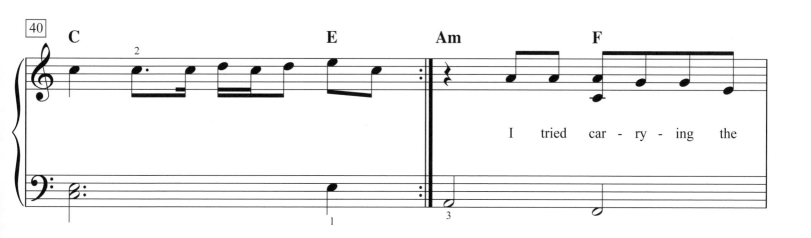

I tried car - ry - ing the

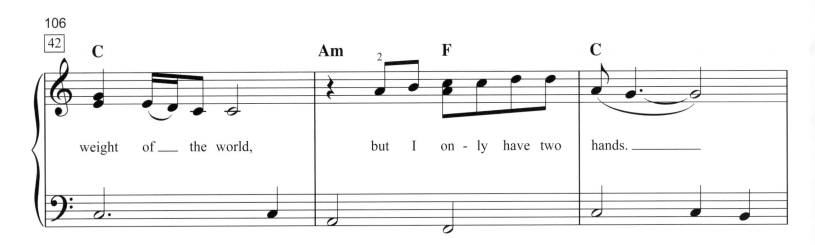

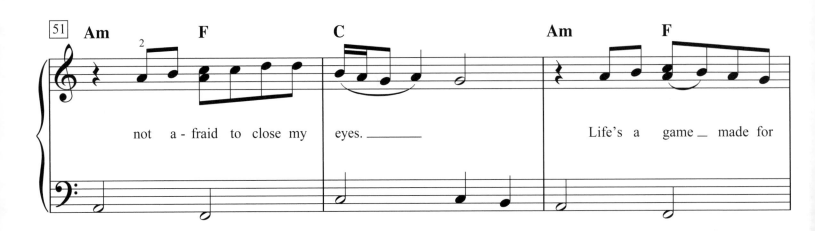

ev - 'ry - one   and love is the   prize. __   So wake me

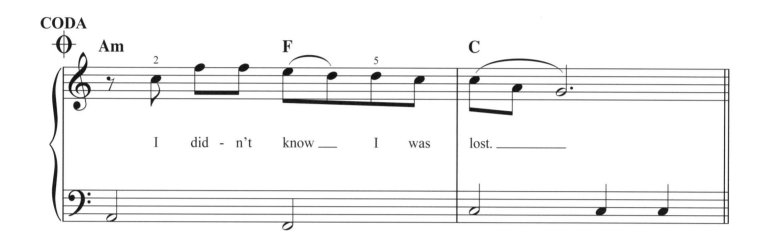

I did - n't know __ I was   lost. _____

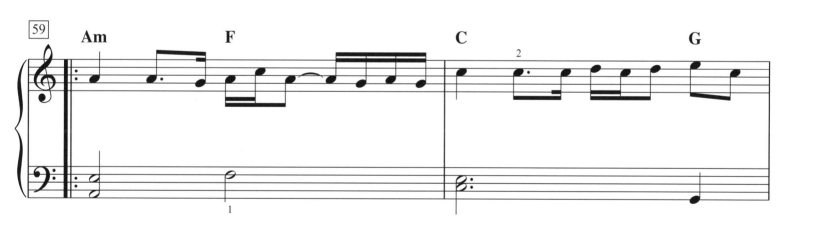

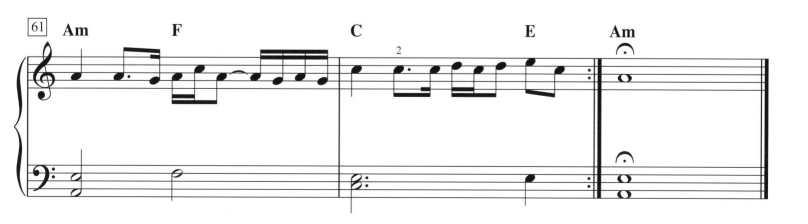

You're My Best Friend

Words and Music by
JOHN DEACON

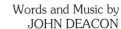
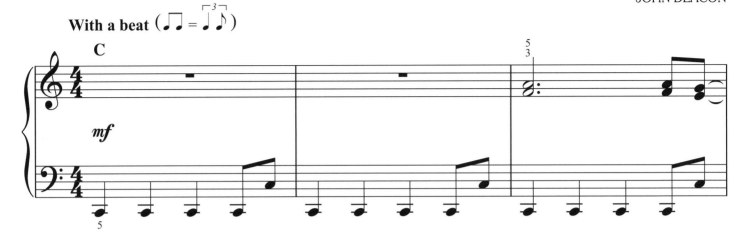

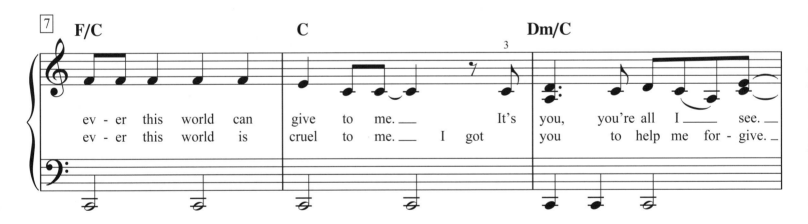
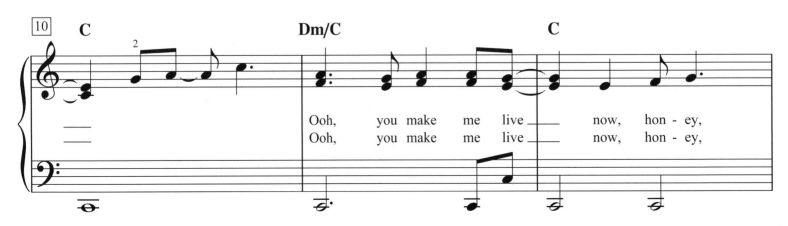

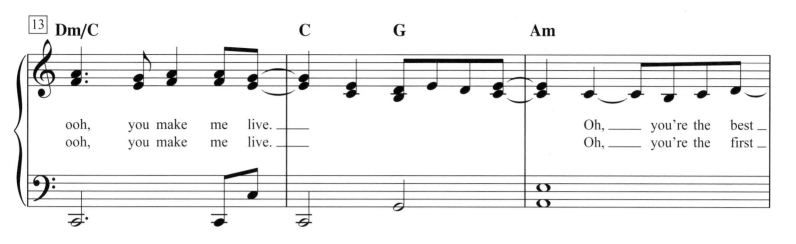

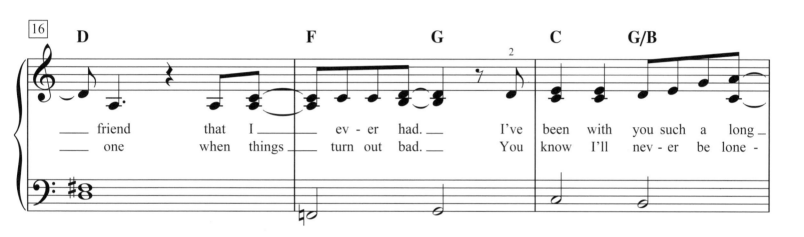

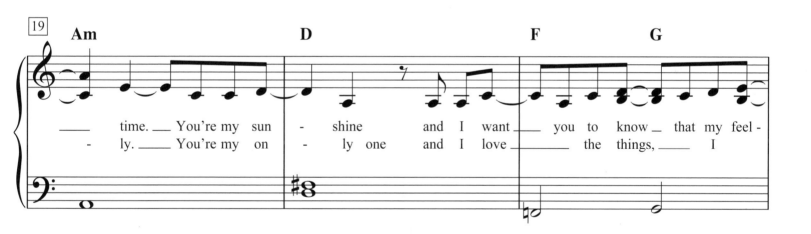

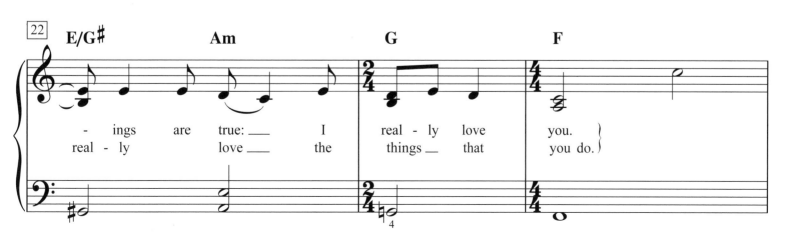

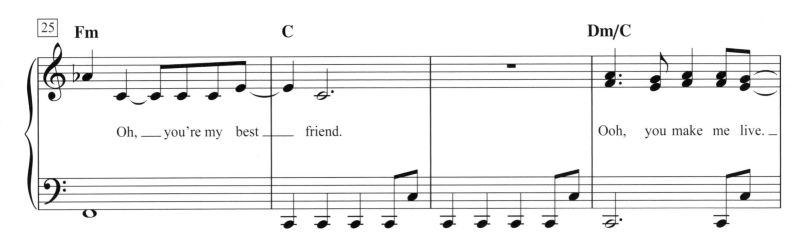

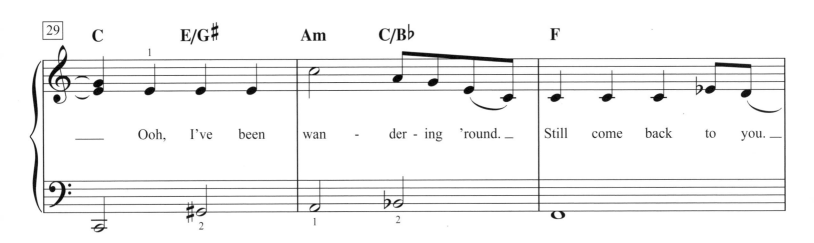

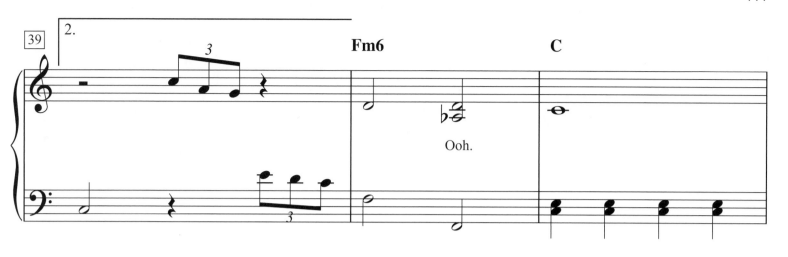

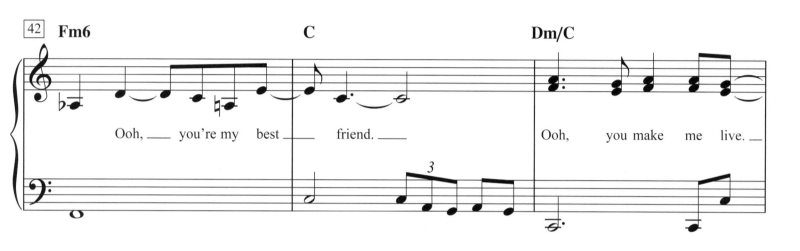

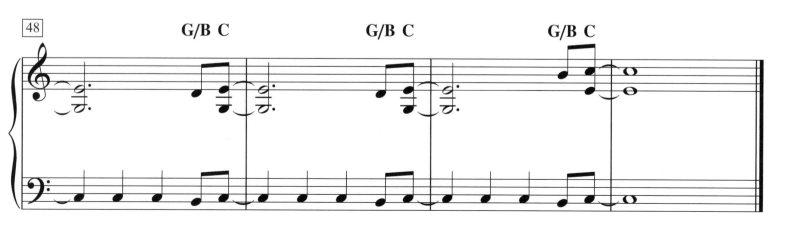

SIMPLE SONGS

THE TITLE SAYS IT ALL: The easiest easy piano arrangements with lyrics to make even beginners sound great! Songs in each collection are carefully chosen to work in these streamlined arrangements.

SIMPLE SONGS

Play 50 of your favorite songs in the easiest of arrangements! Enjoy pop hits, Broadway showstoppers, movie themes, jazz standards, folk tunes and classical melodies presented simply, with lyrics. You'll find something for everyone! Songs include: Beyond the Sea • Castle on a Cloud • Do-Re-Mi • Happy Birthday to You • Hey Jude • Let It Go • Linus and Lucy • Moon River • Ode to Joy • Over the Rainbow • Puff the Magic Dragon • Smile • Star Wars (Main Theme) • Tomorrow • When I Fall in Love • Yesterday • and more.
00142041.. $16.99

(MORE) SIMPLE SONGS

The first edition of our "easiest of easy piano songs" collection was such a success that we found 50 more favorite songs in the easiest of arrangements presented simply, with lyrics. Songs include: All of Me • Brave • Crazy • Danny Boy • Edelweiss • Für Elise • Hallelujah • It's a Small World • Lean on Me • Music Box Dancer • The Pink Panther • Sing • This Land Is Your Land • Unchained Melody • You Raise Me Up • and more.
00172308.. $16.99

SIMPLE BROADWAY SONGS

Play 50 of your favorite songs in the easiest of arrangements! Enjoy Broadway showstoppers presented simply, with lyrics. You'll find something for everyone! Songs include: Dancing Queen · Defying Gravity · Edelweiss · Let It Go · Mama, I'm a Big Girl Now · My Shot · The Music of the Night · Puttin' on the Ritz · Seasons of Love · When I Grow Up · And more!
00295064.. $16.99

SIMPLE CHRISTMAS CAROLS

Play 50 classic carols in the easiest of arrangements, presented simply, with lyrics. Includes: Away in a Manger • Deck the Hall • The First Noel • Go, Tell It on the Mountain • Hark! The Herald Angels Sing • It Came upon the Midnight Clear • Jingle Bells • O Holy Night • Silent Night • The Twelve Days of Christmas • What Child Is This? • and more.
00278263.. $14.99

SIMPLE CHRISTMAS SONGS

Play 50 well-loved holiday songs in the easiest of arrangements! Enjoy classic and contemporary favorites presented simply, with lyrics. Songs include: All I Want for Christmas Is My Two Front Teeth • Blue Christmas • Christmas Time Is Here • Feliz Navidad • Grandma Got Run over by a Reindeer • Have Yourself a Merry Little Christmas • It's Beginning to Look like Christmas • Jingle Bell Rock • Let It Snow! Let It Snow! Let It Snow! • The Most Wonderful Time of the Year • Nuttin' for Christmas • Rudolph the Red-Nosed Reindeer • Santa Claus Is Comin' to Town • Winter Wonderland • You're All I Want for Christmas • and more.
00237197.. $16.99

SIMPLE CLASSICAL PIANO PIECES

Play 50 favorites by Bach, Beethoven, Mozart and others that are perfect for beginners. Pieces include: Minuet in G Major, BWV Appendix 116 • Arabesque from *25 Progressive Studies*, Op. 100, No. 2 • Aria in D minor • Russian Song from *Album for the Young*, Op. 39, No. 11 • Dance in G Major • and more.
00288045.. $9.99

SIMPLE DISNEY SONGS

Play 50 favorite Disney songs in the easiest of arrangements! Enjoy these classic and contemporary selections presented simply, with lyrics. Songs include: Almost There • The Bare Necessities • I've Got a Dream • If I Didn't Have You • Just Around the Riverbend • Let's Go Fly a Kite • Love Is an Open Door • Once upon a Dream • Reflection • Seize the Day • Under the Sea • When You Wish upon a Star • and more.
00355319.. $19.99
Disney characters and artwork (c) & TM 2021 Disney

SIMPLE JAZZ SONGS

Play 50 of your favorite songs in the easiest of arrangements! Enjoy jazz standards presented simply, with lyrics. You'll find something for everyone! Songs include: As Time Goes By • Blue Moon • Here's That Rainy Day • It Had to Be You • Love Is Here to Stay • Mack the Knife • The Nearness of You • On Green Dolphin Street • Sing, Sing, Sing • Someone to Watch Over Me • Sweet Georgia Brown • You'd Be So Nice to Come Home To • and more.
00355461.. $17.99

SIMPLE MOVIE SONGS

Play 50 favorite movie songs in the easiest of arrangements! Enjoy songs from a variety of genres presented simply in easy piano arrangements with lyrics. Includes: Born Free • Cups (When I'm Gone) (from *Pitch Perfect*) • Dawn (from *Pride & Prejudice*) • Endless Love • Gabriel's Oboe (from *The Mission*) • If I Only Had a Brain (from *The Wizard of Oz*) • James Bond Theme • A Million Dreams (from *The Greatest Showman*) • Theme from New York, New York • The Pink Panther • Shallow (from *A Star Is Born*) • Time Warp (from *Rocky Horror Picture Show*) • and many more.
00295065.. $16.99

Browse more products and order today from your favorite music retailer at
halleonard.com

Prices, contents and availability subject to change without notice.